EXPECT THE UNEXPECTED WHEN YOU'RE EXPECTING!

EXPECT THE UNEXPECTED WHEN YOU'RE EXPECTING!

Eunice Glick,
Mindee Glick Garcia, Ph.D.,
and Bonnie Glick MacGinnis

HarperPerennial
A Division of HarperCollinsPublishers

This book is a parody of *What to Expect When You're Expecting* by
Arlene Eisenberg, Heidi E. Murkoff, and Sandee E. Hathaway, B.S.N.,
published by Workman Publishing Company, Inc.

HarperCollins books may be purchased for educational, business, or sales
promotional use. For information please write: Special Markets Depart-
ment, HarperCollins Publishers, Inc., 10 East 53rd Street, New York,
NY 10022.

Text design and illustrations by Nava Atlas

FIRST EDITION

Library of Congress Cataloging-in-Publication Data

Glick, Eunice.
    Expect the unexpected when you're expecting : a hilarious look at the
trials and tribulations of pregnancy, with dozens of exceedingly accurate
drawings and diagrams / by Eunice Glick, Mindee Glick Garcia, &
Bonnie Glick MacGinnis.
        p.   cm.
    This book is a satire on 'What to expect when you're expecting.'
    Includes bibliographical references (p.   ) and index.
    ISBN 0-06-095135-4
    1. Pregnancy—Humor.   I. Garcia, Mindee Glick.   II. MacGinnis,
Bonnie Glick.   III. Eisenberg, Arlene.   What to expect when you're
expecting.   IV. Title.
PN6231.P68G54   1995
618.2'4—dc20   95-32341

95 96 97 98 99 RRD 10 9 8 7 6 5 4 3 2

For Adam and Evan,
always the most unexpectedly wonderful inspirations

Thanks to Patrice Connolly for helping make this project happen; to Eamon Dolan for his brilliant guidance; to H.C.T. for always being there when the boys and I need him; and last but not least, to those of my friends who shared their funniest pregnancy anecdotes, and those who agreed to assume ridiculous poses for some of these illustrations. You know who you are; names have been omitted to protect the innocent!

CONTENTS

FOREWORD

A Word to the Wise by Irwin Glick, Certified Public Accountant

● ●

As far as I'm concerned, there are only two certainties in life—birth and taxes. My somewhat capable (if rather eccentric) cousins are here to advise you on the former, while I am here to give you some pithy pointers on the latter. I ar-

Cousin Irwin urges you to take tax matters seriously! But bear in mind that he's always been a stuffed shirt, and that most of his relatives would rather have oral surgery than spend an evening with him.

gued with Eunice for more space for my commentary, but, stubborn mule that she is (and has always been!), she refused. No wonder Grandma Gilda Glick, Aunt Sonia Potash, and the Glattstein twins no longer speak to her!

But I digress. Look for my handy tax tips at the start of the section on each trimester and highlight them with a yellow marker. Mark my words, they will be the only thing that keeps you from selling this book for a dime at your next garage sale. Take that, Eunice.

And now, on to the critical issue of financial planning as it pertains to family planning: The next time you find yourself in the midst of unprotected sex (whether you do so intentionally or are just too swept up in passion to fumble around for prophylactic devices), ask yourself the following questions:

❑ How can we handle the finances of a growing family when

we barely have enough time to balance our checkbook?

❑ Can we continue to live way beyond our means on only one income?

❑ How many dependents does it take to change a light bulb?

I hope you understand what I'm trying to get at. And if you do, please write to me and explain it, because I am totally lost. What do I know about writing a foreword to a pregnancy guide? I only have two sons myself, and like other men of my generation, I wasn't allowed to be present at their birth. Nor was I there while they were growing up—I was always out busting my chops trying to make a living. Now they expect me to pay for their therapy, which is really not so bad, since I can then claim them as dependents and deduct their psychologist's fees.

But enough about my problems. This book is about you and your impending pregnancy and birth—so go, be fruitful, and multiply. Babies may not be the biggest tax deductions that ever came down the pike, but they certainly are the cutest.

INTRODUCTION

Who We Are and Why You Should Listen to Us

Greetings from the Glicks! Let us introduce ourselves:

Eunice Glick (library school graduation photo, late Eisenhower era), widowed; retired school librarian, mother of coauthors Mindee and Bonnie.

Mindee Glick Garcia, Ph.D. (at age eighteen months, doing her first scientific experiment), molecular physicist; head of Stamppford University's Atomic Research Lab; mother of three.

Bonnie Glick Mac-Ginnis (at high school cheerleading practice, sometime during the last decade or so), probational graduate of Salinas Valley Beauty Academy; mother of two.

Between us, we have given birth seven times, attended ninety-six baby showers, and read twenty-seven sizzling novels that contain birth scenes. In addition, when Bonnie was twelve, she saw a foal being born at the state fair. In other words, we *know* it all, because we've *seen* it all, and therefore are uniquely qualified to dispense advice.

Okay, so it may not always be the most accurate or authoritative advice; in fact this book is bloated with inconsistency, gossip, superstition, and unsubstantiated opinions. But most people relate to this better than they do to dry, scientific data.

We also think that pregnant women have somehow been led to believe that pregnancy is a time for worry, fear, and discomfort. Existing literature only fuels their terror by giving them ideas for more things to worry about. It becomes a vicious cycle of read/ worry, worry/read, worry, worry, worry.

Lighten up! Yours is the eleventeen trillionth pregnancy since the time the Neanderthals officially made the switch to *Homo sapiens*; it's a normal, natural, and wonderful stage in the cycle of life.

After all, the end result is a beautiful baby who will deprive you of sleep, wreck your home and car, and milk you for millions of dollars' worth of educational costs, software, and shoes, but who will also enrich your life like nothing else can. At least that's the idea in theory. And just as with other experiences that seem sort of funky when you are going through them, one day, you will look back on your pregnancy and laugh. Really, you will. We'd just like to give you a head start.

EXPECT THE UNEXPECTED WHEN YOU'RE EXPECTING!

Part One

1

So, Are You or Aren't You, or What?

Early Pregnancy
—Reporter—

You might be pregnant—how exciting! Do you have any idea how this might have happened, or have your long years of casual lovemaking completely disconnected you from the concept of procreative sex? Have you forgotten the deeper meaning behind those anatomical charts that you and your friends snickered over during your fifth grade hygiene assembly?

Today's schools don't give hygiene assemblies any longer (nor does anyone use euphemisms like "hygiene" to describe "the birds and the bees"), since children can now get their entire sex education right from interactive CD-ROMs. But no matter how one learns the scientific facts of conception, the details become a fuzzy blur by the time it actually happens to you. You *do* want to know exactly what happens at the miraculous moment of conception, don't you? Well, let us refresh your memory.

In our opinion, there's nothing more tasteless than those blown-up photos of one helpless, immobile egg being attacked by zillions of sperm. Those tadpolelike tails—ugh! We trust that our readers are sophisticated enough to appreciate the diagram below, which describes the process with a subtle analogy.

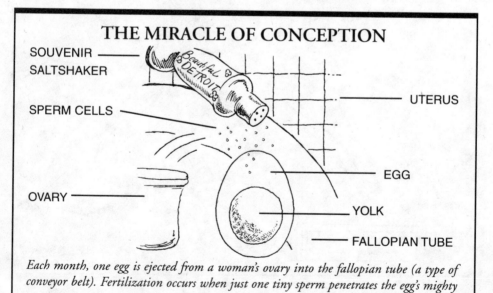

THE MIRACLE OF CONCEPTION

SOUVENIR SALTSHAKER

SPERM CELLS

OVARY

UTERUS

EGG

YOLK

FALLOPIAN TUBE

Each month, one egg is ejected from a woman's ovary into the fallopian tube (a type of conveyor belt). Fertilization occurs when just one tiny sperm penetrates the egg's mighty walls. If you listen carefully, you will hear a quick little "THWUPPP!" when contact is made.

ARE YOU PREGNANT, OR HAVE YOU BEEN MOUNTAIN BIKING?

This handy chart lists the most common early signs of pregnancy; but since women's bodies are temples of unexplained phenomena, there may be reasons other than pregnancy for these same symptoms.

COMMON EARLY SYMPTOM OF PREGNANCY	POSSIBLE CAUSE OF SYMPTOM OTHER THAN PREGNANCY
Missed period	Leap year; mountain biking
Tender gums	Gingivitis; plaque
Broccoli and other vegetables taste strange	Vegetables are spoiled or overcooked
Frequent urination	Sangria; gallons of Gatorade
Sore breasts	Bad underwire; clumsy husband or lover
Morning sickness	Hangover; salmonella; indigestion

**This is so important to know that you
should read it and commit it to memory at once!**

HOW TO USE THE HOME PREGNANCY TEST

• •

Wow! You have most of the early pregnancy symptoms on the preceding chart, do you? And you haven't been mountain biking, swilling sangria, or cooking rotten vegetables. Now what?

Most women take a home pregnancy test in the privacy of their own bathroom before starting a search for an obstetrician. Nothing is worse than being sent home from the OB's office for false pregnancy, except being sent home from the hospital for false labor. Here's what you do:

1. Go to the pharmacy, buy a home pregnancy test kit. Pay for it with a shy smile, eyes lowered.

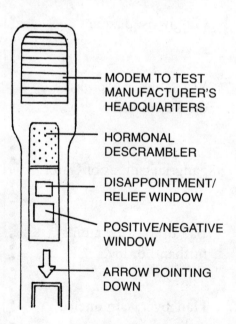

MODEM TO TEST
MANUFACTURER'S
HEADQUARTERS

HORMONAL
DESCRAMBLER

DISAPPOINTMENT/
RELIEF WINDOW

POSITIVE/NEGATIVE
WINDOW

ARROW POINTING
DOWN

2. Read the instructions, which usually say to use your first urine of the morning to conduct the test. Look at your watch. It is 5:30 P.M.

3. You can't wait till morning—you're just too curious. Go to your bathroom, assemble the test kit, pee on this magical piece of plastic and cotton, and wait for the appropriate symbol (usually a stripe or a plus sign) to appear. Nothing happens—no positive sign, no negative sign. See? You really must wait until morning. If you can't follow such simple instructions, how do you expect to take care of a baby?

4. Go back to the pharmacy, buy another home pregnancy test kit. Same cashier as before. Pay for it with an embarrassed smile, eyes totally averted.

5. Go home, vow to follow the instructions this time. Before going to bed, assemble the kit and place it on the toilet lid. Toss and turn all night. Finally get up at 5:00 A.M., figuring that this has to count as morning already. Pee on the tester and wait. Could it be? There it is, the positive sign!

6. Pick up the phone and call your friends, even thought it's 5:08 A.M.; after all, **YOU ARE PREGNANT!** Prepare a press release to send to all the local papers. Finally, don't forget to wake up the lucky father-to-be with the exciting news.

IN LESS THAN NINE MONTHS, YOU ARE GOING TO BE NEW PARENTS!

You'll be responsible for a fragile, delicate existence—yours. After all, you're the ones facing a major life change, not the baby. Babies are actually the most resilient little suckers on the face of the earth.

ONCE YOU ARE SURE THAT YOU'RE PREGNANT...

❑ Cancel your subscriptions to upscale lifestyle and fashion magazines like *Condé Nast Traveler, Gourmet,* and *Elle.* They are now useless, as well as frustrating. Instead, take out subscriptions to practical, nuts-and-bolts publications like *Parents, Working Mother,* and *Good Housekeeping.*

❑ Buy your man a copy of *Puttering Pete's 101 Home Furniture-Making Projects for the Weekend Workbench Warrior.* It's chock-full of projects to occupy him once he gives up his personal vices in preparation for daddyhood. Perhaps he can make a crude, amateurish cradle or a rocking chair that you will never actually use.

❑ Get married, if you haven't done so already. Call me (Eunice) old-fashioned, but I think a baby should be born into a sanctified union, like Mindee's marriage to Enrico Ruiz Garcia, M.D., the last in a long line of Spanish-Jewish anesthesiologists. However, even a sham of a marriage, like Bonnie's to "Wee Wanderin' Willie," is better than none at all.

❑ Take an inventory of your bank account, investments, your parents' nest egg, plus your wallet and coupon drawer. Then study our section on "The Nesting Syndrome: Exactly How Much Will It Cost You?" (page 38). After taking these steps, you and your mate might each consider getting a second job.

CHOOSING THE PERFECT PRACTITIONER AND PERSONAL PSYCHIC FOR YOUR PREGNANCY

Most women spend more time and effort finding a hairstylist than they do the right practitioner for their pregnancies. A pity, because a bad haircut will always grow out, but a bad experience with an OB or midwife will remain forever etched in your mind. Choose an obstetrician or midwife who:

❑ Has a personalized license plate that reads BABYDOC.

❑ Employs nurses that don't make snorting sounds when they weigh you.

❑ Doesn't automatically prescribe every prenatal test ever invented, no matter what your age or circumstances.

❑ Has delivered at least six thousand babies (and hangs pictures of most of them all over the office) but still treats you as if your pregnancy is somehow unique and special in all the world.

❑ Decorates his or her office with chintz fabrics and country accessories.

❑ Promises to allow you to have pain relief if you want it, but will not force it on you if you are enjoying your contractions.

❑ (And this is very important) Considers your current insurance coverage a legitimate form of payment.

Avoid the following practitioners:

The "new age" obstetrician (male or female): Potentially a good choice for women planning to go the "natural" way, what with the whale song tapes they play in their office. Be aware of this practitioner's downsides, though: a tendency toward too much wisecracking (during office visits *and* labor), and a hint of smugness if you decide, at the last minute, that you *do* want pain relief, after all.

The "old-school" male obstetrician: This geezer, whose bedside manner consists of a repulsive, lizardlike touch and a smarmy attitude, actively dislikes women and treats pregnancy as a disease.

The less-than-sympathetic female practitioner: Rarely, but it does happen, female OBs or midwives who've had easy births themselves, or haven't given birth at all, can be less empathetic with the mother-to-be than an average male practitioner. Expect comments like "Snap out of it!" and "Come on, you can make it to the next contraction!"

WHY YOU NEED A PERSONAL PSYCHIC

Why a psychic? Face it—you're leaping into a cosmic void with this pregnancy business. You *must* get a handle on the future, and the best way to do this is with a psychic. Any kind will do—tarot card reader, astrologer, palmist, crystal ball interpreter. For pregnancy, we strongly recommend using a female who uses the title of "Mrs." on her sign, as in "Mrs. Gina, Faymus Palm Readr I Wil Tell Yer Fewcher, Only $65." Bonnie used Mrs. Gina and swears by her. If she hadn't consulted with Mrs. Gina during her last pregnancy, she would have been totally unprepared for her husband's fling with that management consultant slut.

Part Two

2
THE MOST-LIKELY DIET

Food, glorious food. Gobs and gobs of food. Mountains, rivers, oceans of it. That's one of the perks of being pregnant in this day and age. You're allowed to eat and enjoy, unlike when I, Eunice, was pregnant in the 1950s. Back in those dark days, doctors warned our generation of Stepford Wives not to gain more than fifteen pounds during pregnancy. Fifteen pounds! Why, that's barely enough weight gain to accommodate a six- or seven-pound baby, the placenta, and a little extra mucous.

While there's no need to go so overboard with food that you'll have to be moved about with a fork lift, isn't it nice to know that no one bats an eyelash over a thirty-five-pound weight gain anymore? Ah, what I could have done with thirty-five pounds! So listen, take the old saw of "eating for two" a step further—eat for three: yourself, the baby, and me, Eunice. I can only live vicariously through my adorable readers.

WHAT IS THE "MOST-LIKELY" DIET, ANYWAY?

Reflecting how expectant women are *most likely* to eat throughout their pregnancy, this diet is based on hearsay, mangled facts, and stories of alien births from supermarket tabloids. It follows the dictates of desire rather than the shackles of common sense and good nutrition. Do we actually *recommend* the Most-Likely Diet? Not a chance. However, the following patterns are common to everyone whose arm we twisted for the truth about chowing down during pregnancy.

❑   **The first trimester** is dominated by the need to quell the queasies. The appetite is often dull, and many everyday foods suddenly smell and taste awfully strange. It's true—pickles and ice cream (separately, not together as myth would have it) are comforting, as are other sour tastes and, of course, crackers—especially saltines.

❑   **The second trimester** is chow time! You're hungry every minute of every waking hour. You'll also begin to experience those amusing cravings that pregnant women are famous for. Blessed is she who lives near a twenty-four-hour deli, for she shall eat and be merry.

❏ **The third trimester** begins as a seamless segue of the second, then, around the eighth month, women are seized by a need for truckloads of protein. In very late pregnancy, the stomach gets squished by the body's blossoming tenant, which tempers a hefty appetite with bouts of indigestion and heartburn.

EXPLODING THE "PICKLES AND ICE CREAM" MYTH:
The Lowdown on Cravings

Pregnant women really *do* crave pickles and ice cream in gangbuster quantities, but we have yet to meet anyone who has craved them at the same time. This is just a myth that has persisted since the "I Love Lucy" era, along with the idea that pregnancy instantly transforms women into daffy dimwits.

And so, dismissed as fluffbrains, our cravings are mocked and scorned, which is not the case in more sophisticated parts of the world like Borneo and Yalta, and among savvy folk as the Hottentots and Sherpas.

In these enlightened societies, a pregnant woman's cravings (sometimes called "fancies") are sacred. To deny her desires invites the "evil eye," six-headed giants, and other unwanted company. The expectant mother's mate wouldn't hesitate to travel for forty miles on foot to obtain an obscure berry that she craves, or he would cross dangerous, viper-infested rivers to reach a tree with superior coconuts.

Don't be timid about getting your cravings satisfied, no matter how bizarre or expensive they may be. For example: Do you absolutely *have* to have fresh portobello mushrooms, grilled to perfection with aged Gorgonzola cheese, or you'll die? If your man really cares for the woman who is spawning his seed, he would be resourceful with this kind of tricky craving: He would find a log, put it in a damp spot, spray it with portobello cultures and grow the portobellos himself so he can harvest them any time you desire. Then he would scour the area for an authentic Italian deli in search of a perfectly aged wedge of Gorgonzola, fire up the stovetop grill, and put the whole shebang together artfully on a lovely piece of Limoges china. Now that's true love!

There's no time better than this to test your man's devotion and at the same time let loose with your fondest food fantasies! Be creative with your cravings, and don't be a slave to the clock: three A.M. is as good a time for a "gotta have it" as any other time (You: Honey, wake up! I've really gotta have some mock turtle soup! Him: Mmf, I'm up! I'm up!) If you can't think of anything more exotic than rocky road ice cream to beg your man to bring you in the middle of the night, here are some suggestions to get your salivary glands going:

❑ A towering macaroni pie encircled with champignons.

❑ Bread and milk and freshly picked blackberries with chamomile tea, à la Peter Rabbit, Flopsy, Mopsy, and Cottontail.

❑ Imported pâté de foie gras in aspic, vegetarian-style.

❑ Oysters Rockefeller on points of toast with Grapes Flambée Vanderbilt.

❑ Chestnuts roasted on an open fire (this will be a particularly challenging craving for your mate to help you satisfy if it occurs in spring or summer).

❑ Freshly baked twenty-four-grain bread, served with a quart of seedless pomegranate jelly (guess which lucky guy has to grind the grains and pit the pomegranates?).

You get the idea. Happy eating, and send us any really unique recipes that you or your fella come up with, and we'll include them in our sequel, *What to Gorge Yourself Senseless on When You're Expecting.*

IS IT ME, OR DOES THE RUTABAGA SMELL WEIRD?

Since pregnancy is traditionally equated with insatiable gluttony, many newly expectant women are alarmed by their poor appetite. Many foods become downright offensive; this can be blamed on hormonal changes (we can blame an awful lot of things on hormones, can't we?) that affect a pregnant woman's sense of smell. This, in turn, alters the perception of how we think a food will taste.

Happily, this phenomenon passes, usually by the beginning of the fourth month, at which time these and all the other foods on earth will appeal to you more than ever before. The foods listed below are considered the most unpalatable during the first trimester:

OFFENDING FOOD	WHAT IT MAY SMELL LIKE TO YOU IN YOUR FIRST TRIMESTER
Beans	A damp, mildewy basement
Broccoli	Sulfuric acid
Corn-on-the-cob	Ammonia
Chinese food	Rush-hour traffic fumes in Beijing
Garlic	The filthy laundry of a marathon runner
Crabs, lobster, men-of-war, and other sea creatures	Turpentine

RECIPES FOR THE FIRST TRIMESTER:
Soothing Mister Nausea

• •

CRACKER MÉLANGE WITH PRECIOUS BABY GREENS

Serves 1 pregnant person twice

These bitsy greens are delicate, like your appetite, and pricey—but baby, you're worth it!

½ pound mixed baby lettuces (those exotic lettuce leaves sold by gourmet produce stores in cellophane containers for about $15.99 a pound)
½ cup crushed saltines
½ cup crushed matzo
½ cup melba toast or zwieback, cracked with a hammer
Lemon juice

For each serving, place the baby lettuces in a bowl and sprinkle on some of the crushed crackers and lemon juice. Eat while dreamily looking at a nursery furnishings catalog, then lay down for a nap.

PICKLED RINDS EL SUPREMO

Makes about 17 gallons

A steady diet of pickles can grow boring, but not only cucumber pickles qualify as part of a nausea-quelling diet. Pickles can be made of any fruit or vegetable, according to the *Old Farmer's Almanac of Inaccurate Weather Predictions, Bucolic Hokum, and Canning Recipes.* But the very best pickles are made of the rinds of produce. And the stomach upset they cause will completely overshadow any little bouts of queasiness.

Rinds of 8 watermelons
Rinds of 6 honeydew melons
Rinds of 4 acorn squashes
Rinds of 4 grapefruits
Rinds of a dozen oranges
10 gallons vinegar
1 cup mixed pickling spices

Combine all the ingredients in a clean bathtub and let stand overnight. Transfer to sterilized canning jars and seal hermetically.

RECIPES FOR THE SECOND TRIMESTER:
Looking for Mister Good Food

● ●

FETTUCCINE FOUR SEASONS AND EIGHT CHEESES
(Otto Formaggi)

Serves 1 pregnant person generously, plus 10 to 12 regular people moderately

From the kitchens of *Il Carciofo Schifo* ("The Dirty Artichoke"), Milan's premier grubbery, comes this lavish recipe. It's decidedly *not* for calorie-counters!

1 pound fettuccine pasta, scrubbed, cooked, and drained
1 cup expensive wild forest mushrooms, hacked to smithereens
1 pint extremely heavy cream
1 cup Parmesan cheese, recently grated
1 cup Gorgonzola cheese, crumbled
1 cup Reggiano cheese, galvanized
½ cup mozzarella cheese, scored and slivered
4 ounces goat cheese, cut into tiny, pizza-shaped wedges
½ cup Fontina cheese, grated into very long shreds with a carrot peeler or manual pencil sharpener
½ cup Brie, whipped soundly
4 ounces soft cream cheese, squeezed from a pastry tube

Combine all the ingredients in an attractive pasta bowl. Serve with salad and a garnish of lactose-digesting enzyme tablets.

TRIPLE CHOCOLATE FREAK-OUT

We prefer to leave the number of portions up to you so that you don't blame us for any ill effects

Adapted from an upscale cooking magazine that doesn't dare give nutritional breakdowns for fear of being sued by cardiac patients, this is so indulgent, so rich, and so sinful that the act of devouring it borders on the metaphysical.

The cake layer:

Six packages Hostess chocolate cupcakes (12 cupcakes altogether, in case you're too spaced out to multiply), minced

The ganache layer:

1 pound box Godiva (or equivalent) chocolates
12-ounce package M & M's
1 cup café-quality cappuccino

Buttercream frosting, or cholesterol layer:

2 cups whipping cream, beaten until it forms peaks the size of small dogs
12 egg yolks, beaten and simmered until they have
the color and flavor of Greek lemons
4 sticks (1 pound) butter, wrapping paper intact

Put the minced cupcakes into a cake pan and smoosh them in until the crumbs stick together, almost like real cake.

Melt the items for the ganache layer in a saucepan, then pour over the cake layer. Top with the smoothly combined beaten whipping cream, egg yolks, and mocha beans. Garnish with the wrapped butter sticks arranged geometrically on top (we aren't sure whether you are actually supposed to eat any part of the butter, since Bonnie accidentally poured squid ink over that part of the recipe in the magazine).

You're supposed to chill this for several hours, but given your appetite, go ahead and dig in at once.

Friendly tip: For the next few days, have two or three nice, big bowls of cooked oat bran for breakfast to counteract the effects of the buttercream frosting, especially if you ate the butter.

RECIPES FOR THE THIRD TRIMESTER:
Feeding Mister Protein Monster

• •

SUPER-SOY EXTRA-DELIGHT GRANOLA
Serves 4 pregnant people

An excellent, protein-packed breakfast choice for Earth Mothers (see page 63), or anyone seeking an antidote to the previous recipe.

2 pounds field-picked organic soybeans
1 pound each extra-firm and super-firm tofu
4 cups granola cereal
4 cups vanilla n' ginseng-flavored soymilk
6 links tofu "hot dogs," sliced
4 large onions, drawn and quartered

Rinse the soybeans and pick over, checking for chunks of dirt and debris, small rocks, and scrap metal.

Cover with water, then uncover. Cover. Uncover. Cover. Bring to an angry boil, then lower the heat and cook for several hours, or until the soybeans no longer smell quite so much like sneakers and can be fairly easily pierced with wire cutters. Drain.

Spend the next several hours picking out those yucky little soybean skins that separate from the beans during cooking. Then, puree the soybeans together with the tofus (or is it tofi?).

To assemble, divide the granola among four bowls and pour the soymilk over it. Ladle on a generous glob of the soybean-tofu puree, then top each serving with a smattering of tofu hot dog slices and onions. Yum!

CAPTAIN JACK'S BARNACLE GUMBO
Serves 4 pregnant people or 16 regular people

Our cousin Elaine recently cruised aboard a schooner to Caribbean ports of call. She loved this recipe so much that she wheedled it from Captain Jack, who she described as a naughty and very salty sea dog. Elaine promises that it is luscious, but since she's the Glick family's pathological liar, we passed on testing it. We include it only because a single serving of barnacles has more protein than a whole side of beef.

3 pounds freshly scraped barnacles, preferably from the hull of a forty-foot schooner
2 pounds scallops, scalloped
1 pound extremely young okra pods, stemmed, halved, and vigorously rinsed of slime

29-ounce can "clamato" juice cocktail, opened
2 tablespoons Chef Rudehomme's Hotter-n'-Tarnation Cajun Seasoning
Heaps and heaps of hot cooked white rice

Combine the ingredients, except the rice, in an industrial-sized stew pot. Cook for two hours, or until the barnacles are just springy to the tooth. Heap over mounds of white rice in large bowls.

Part Three

3

THE FIRST TRIMESTER

People to call, Continued:

Zelda Glattstein
Arabelle Glick
Sandra O'Donnell Glick
Sidney Q. Glick
Grandma Gilda Glick
Annette Price Glick
Shirley Glick
Rhonda ~~~~ Glick
Irwin Glick
Janet Glick
Ashley T. Glick
Andrea Glidstein
Sharon Glimberg
Susan Glimcher

...AND I'M 7.275 WEEKS PREGNANT, AND JEFFREY SAYS...AND...

QUEASE N' CRACKERS

EXPECT THE UNEXPECTED AT YOUR FIRST PRENATAL CHECKUP

• •

Your first visit to the obstetrician will be a delicate, touchy experience. You can expect to feel vulnerable, even slightly humiliated. And you're still in the *waiting room*! All those medical forms; all those personal, personal questions…

Expect to complete a checklist on which of your relatives has had emphysema, ringworm, lice, massive clots, hysteria, and every other physical and mental disease ever known. But you need not reveal *every* skeleton in your family closet, as Bonnie did when she was expecting her first child. In the space for "other family diseases" she wrote that Great-Grandma Ruth Potash once contracted rabies from an angry squirrel.

Naturally, your own medical history as well as your personal habits (Do you smoke? Drink? Shop compulsively? Is your period regular? NO? why not?) won't escape scrutiny.

Expect to be marched to the desk of a steely-eyed woman who reminds you of your seventh grade gym teacher; she will grill you on the extent and legitimacy of your insurance coverage.

Expect, for once, to crave your practitioner's poking and prodding, so you can hear that sweet affirmation, "By golly, you really *are* pregnant!"

$ $ $ $ $ $ $ $ $ $ $ $ $

IRWIN GLICK'S TAX TIPS FOR THE FIRST TRIMESTER

❑ Feeling that onslaught of emotions common to new moms-to-be? Joy one minute, anxiety the next? Your family financial records are probably in disarray. Get organized *now* and enjoy peace of mind for the remainder of your pregnancy.

❑ Constipated? It's probably because you haven't contributed enough to your Individual Retirement Account. Add to your retirement fund regularly, and you'll be more regular, too.

$ $ $ $ $ $ $ $ $ $ $ $ $

What You Might Look Like This Trimester

NOT AGAIN!
BLURP

By the sixth week of pregnancy, the prune-sized fetus is already wreaking havoc with your hormones. Many newly pregnant women will want to stay close to their favorite sink until well past the third month.

FINAL JEOPARD

PREGNAN PAUSES

Those same hormonal storms leave you with a feeling that can only be described as "cosmic exhaustion." Most of you will be zoned out before "Final Jeopardy."

YOUR FIRST PRENATAL EXAM:

The Waiting-Room Magazine Tolerance Test

While waiting on pins and needles to be called in for your first prenatal exam, your unwitting transformation into a mass consumer of baby goods will begin, thanks to a barrage of waiting-room magazines you never knew existed. Magazines with names like:

❑ **Mommy-to-Be!**
❑ **Anglo-Saxon Baby**
❑ **BabyStyle: The Magazine for Affluent Parents of Tiny Infants**

These magazines all trade the same stock articles back and forth. After skimming them during this and your subsequent visits to your practitioner, you'll notice endless variations on these themes, such as:

❑ *"How to Feel Less Isolated When You Spend 24 Hours a Day
   With a Colicky Newborn"*

❑ *"Bottle or Breast, Which Is Best, and How to Rationalize the
   Wrong Decision"*

❑ *"When Is the Right Time to Return to Work, If Ever, and How
   to Choose Proper Child Care Without Incredible Guilt and
   Remorse"*

❑ *"Getting Your Infant to Sleep Through the Night—Really.
   No, Really*"

And so on. The articles don't much matter; these publications are mainly vehicles for ads designed to convince you that you just can't get along without battery-powered portable bottle-warmers, fruit-scented teething rings, "developmentally correct" infant toys and mobiles, snack organizers that turn into portable potties (and vice versa), and many other clever items never available to those unfortunate babies born before 1987.

Is it any wonder that the current generation is so angst-ridden? After all, we never had the benefit of "developmentally correct" stimulation such as this lovely mobile.

ESTIMATING YOUR DUE DATE

One of the more exciting events of your first prenatal visit is when your practitioner takes a stab at your "due date." Of course, no one but the baby knows when it will be good and ready to be born. Of what use is a due date to a fetus who is just as liable to pop out a month early as two weeks late? However, you *will* need a handy date to latch on to, since everyone you know (as well as an alarming number of strangers) will ask you when you are due.

The scientific term for "due date" is E.D.C.—Estimated Date of Confinement. Yes, confinement! This term has persisted since Victorian times, when giving birth was considered so shameful that women were literally confined to the most remote room of those big, gloomy houses they lived in back then. It makes us just want to weep all over our fainting sofas!

The simplest way to determine the likely due date is:

Date of conception + 9 months = Due date.

However, insurance companies will not reimburse practitioners who figure out the due date this way. The only way your first prenatal exam will be reimbursable is if your practitioner uses this method:

First day of your Last Menstrual Period (L.M.P.) + 7 days + Degrees of Rotational Axis (D.R.A.) of Earth to Venus + 3 months, minus 2 weeks for Obstetrician's or Midwife's Major Yearly Vacation (O.M.M.Y.V.) = Due date (E.D.C.)

If you totally flubbed the date of the first day of your L.M.P., which most women do, all of this is a bunch of B.S., and that's why 95 percent of all babies are never born on their E.D.C.

VICES YOU WILL HAVE TO GIVE UP AT ONCE

Let's dispense with the obvious—unless you're a complete moron, which you can't be if you have the good sense to be reading this book, you already know that cigarettes, alcohol, and controlled substances are strictly verboten. But what about the finer, more subtle vices in a woman's life? Which ones will you need to learn to do without from here on?

Beautiful satin lingerie: You must now budget for sensible nursing bras in various sizes, as the size of your breasts will change daily according to your baby's appetite.

Fire-engine red lipstick: Inappropriate; leaves stains on baby's tender skin after kissing, and in addition, red lipstick in conjunction with your frazzled-new-mom look will make you look psychotic. Get used to doing without it *now*—the red lipstick habit is hard to break.

Spike-heeled shoes: Forget it! Stash them in the back of your closet, along with your bikini swimsuits. They're totally incompatible with the pregnant body, and dangerous when toting a tiny infant.

Dark, delicious, sinful chocolate: Breastfeeding after you've indulged in chocolate may cause your baby a major tummy-ache. True chocoholics need time to wean themselves from the habit, so start now. Actually, have a nice "farewell to chocolate" bash tonight, and start tomorrow.

Expensive perfumes and colognes: Save your money! There's nothing more intoxicating than a new baby's natural scent, combined with powder, stale milk, and a slightly wet diaper. You wouldn't want to overpower that with any sort of artificial aroma, would you?

WHAT YOU MIGHT BE FRETTING ABOUT ALREADY

• •

TOO YOUNG TO HAVE A BABY?

I'm twenty, and thrilled that I'm going to have a baby. But I'm also concerned; I've barely begun to discover who I am. Will I have the maturity, patience, and stability to raise a child?

Nope.

TOO OLD TO HAVE A BABY?

I'm forty-two, and thrilled that I'm going to have a baby. But I'm also concerned; I'm finally rising to the top of my career. Will I have the time, stamina, and flexibility to raise a child?

Nope.

TOO SOON TO ANNOUNCE MY PREGNANCY?

My home pregnancy test confirms that I'm pregnant. I can't be more than five or six weeks along, but I can't wait to tell everyone I know,

and shout it from the rooftops, too. Is it too early to announce my pregnancy?

In our section on "How to Use the Home Pregnancy Test," we advise the happy mother-to-be to call her friends the moment the pregnancy test shows up positive, even though it's only 5:08 A.M., and prepare press releases for the local media. We trust that our readers are savvy enough to realize that our tongues were planted firmly in our cheeks.

Great-grandmother Ida Rothstein passed down a family tradition that encouraged any expectant mothers in the family to wait until the fragile first three months had passed (see "The Evil Eye," page 53). This was a mere formality, since the women in our family could always tell when someone was pregnant. Suddenly, she turns green at the sight of chopped liver—big secret! But we'd hold our tongues and let the time pass so that the mother-to-be could feel that she was surprising us when she was ready.

We could lecture you from now until the cows come home on

why you should wait to make your announcement until after the third month, but we can tell that you're too anxious and won't listen to us anyway. So go, do what you have to do. We're not the ones who have to pay your phone bill.

WHEN YOUR BREASTS TAKE ON A LIFE OF THEIR OWN

I'm just eight weeks pregnant and I've already grown from an A to a C cup bra, and even that is starting to overflow. My nipples have gotten larger, darker, and bumpier. My breasts always feel tender and tingly, and are criss-crossed with blue veins. I'm not a happy camper. Is there anything I can do?

First of all, thanks for the glorious details. It's a good thing we ate lunch before we read your question. Now, let's break out the violins and hankies. This lady's breasts are doing a bang-up job of preparing themselves for that for which nature has intended them—nursing a baby—and she wants sympathy!

Sure, there's plenty you can do. If you have time to spare, you can volunteer at a soup kitchen or a women's shelter; take up gardening or pottery; put in extra time at work; or make a quilt for your baby. In other words, get your mind out of your bra and occupy it elsewhere.

Modestly endowed women (and their mates) are often delighted when pregnancy makes them voluptuous for the first time in their lives!

Take a day off from work here and there and spend it gazing fondly into the mirror. Enjoy the view while it lasts—before you know it, the protrusion of your belly will soon overtake that of your breasts.

SPORTS TO AVOID NOW AND FOR THE REST OF YOUR PREGNANCY

While no one would dispute the benefits of gentle exercise during pregnancy (prolonged inertia can become permanent), keep in mind that expectant mothers are also entitled to lots of rest. This is not only because resting is more comfy than aerobics, but because you are just months away from giving birth to a small person who will not allow you a moment's rest until it leaves home for college. So exercise gently if you must, but do give up the following, hazardous sports immediately.

SPORT	REASON TO AVOID	SUBSTITUTE ACTIVITY
Scuba diving	Water might be forced into the birth canal	Go to a pet store and look at the fishies
Surfing	Surf might be forced into the birth canal	Take a tepid bubble bath while listening to the Beach Boys
Sky diving	Cloud matter might be forced into the birth canal	Shoot spit-balls from a balcony
Downhill skiing	Snow might be forced into the birth canal	Hire a St. Bernard to haul you up and down a snowy street in a sleigh

IT'S NEVER TOO SOON TO START YOUR "KEGEL" EXERCISES

Every pregnancy expert in the world advocates Kegel exercises. We, too, give Kegels (from the Dutch word for "tights") the Glick Seal of Approval. Here's a quick review on how to do them:

❑ Pretend that you need to pee. Actually, don't pretend, just go pee, since you probably have to, anyway.

❑ In "midstream," so to speak, clench up your vaginal muscles to stop the stream. Then release. Clench. Release. Clench. Release.

❑ Repeat this exercise two thousand times a day throughout your pregnancy. Don't laugh! It strengthens those all-important muscles like nothing else can, and the real beauty of it is that you can do these exercises anywhere—at your desk, during meetings, while driving—and no one will know.

Another benefit of Kegels: becoming good at this exercise might be the closest you come to having decent sex for some time.

• •

THE PARENTAL APTITUDE TEST (P.A.T.)
If you can't pass this test, you're not prepared to be parents!

You're on the precipice of parenthood—a time warp with its own rules and even its own vocabulary. Whether you are a Ph.D. in molecular physics like Mindee, an all-purpose "wannabe" like Bonnie, a vice president of marketing at a major corporation, or a high school dropout peddling earrings in the street, everyone starts at square one when it comes to baby literacy.

Learn to talk the talk! This quiz will help you master a few basics, but you must also start going on research expeditions to Toys "Я" Us and children's bookstores, hanging out at playgrounds to observe and listen, and watching public television on weekday mornings.

1. How much would you be willing to pay a scalper for second-row tickets to a Barney concert?

    a. $29.50 apiece
    b. $342.50 apiece
    c. If my child wanted to see Barney, cost would not be an issue.
    d. Who's Barney?

2. Follow-up question: Who *is* Barney?

    a. The ratlike mascot of a restaurant/arcade chain
    b. A gentle, guitar-strumming troubadour
    c. A large, bouncing, giggling, purple dinosaur. No kidding!
    d. I still have no idea

3. Snuffle-upagus is the imaginary friend of which Sesame Street character?

    a. That angry, antisocial muppet that lives in a trash can
    b. Elmo, the cute little toddler-muppet with the red fur
    c. I know! I know! Big Bird!
    d. I used to watch Sesame Street when I was little, but they didn't have Snuffle-upagus back then

4. Which of the following is an "orthodontically correct" pacifier, which will someday save you thousands of dollars, if you're lucky?

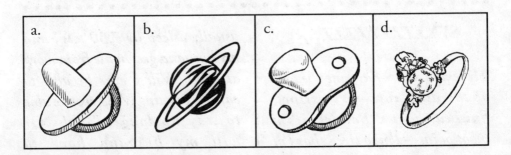

5. Finish the following sentence honestly: For me, there is no more pleasurable way to spend a Saturday morning than...

    a. Shopping for fabulous bargains at the mall

    b. Hiking or going to the health club

    c. Attending a birthday party with a dozen or so rambunctious toddlers at Jumpin' Gene's Gym Jamboree

    d. Sleeping off a tough week at work

6. Which group of domestic items have you been thinking about lately?

    a. Bread machine / juicer / Parmesan cheese grater / French garlic press / espresso machine

    b. Color flatbed scanner / videoRAM / magneto-optical disks / multiport remote access

    c. Safety gate / changing table / deluxe baby dishwasher basket / steam sterilizer / portable playyard

    d. Lint / dust spores / mold / mildew / other allergens

You are prepared for parenthood only if you answered all the questions "c." If you answered with a lot of "a"s and "b"s, you've got a lot to learn. If you answered all the questions "d," you're hopeless and must embark on a crash course in baby literacy if you have any hope of being prepared for what lies ahead.

MORE FRETTING

• •

SEXZZZZZZZZZ...

My sexual desire has gone the way of the dinosaurs—it's extinct, finished, kaput. Besides, it's a moot point—I'm so tired that I'm *usually asleep by 7:30 P.M., and my husband gets home from work at 8:00. Will I ever be able to enjoy sex again? Will I ever be able to stay up long enough? Or will my husband have to accommodate his desires else-where?*

Well, Mrs. E.W. of Covered Bridges, Nebraska, we didn't want to be the ones to bring it up, but why does it take your husband three hours to make the ten-minute trip home after his shift ends at 5:00? Could it be because your "husband's" divorce from Mrs. G.W. of Ball Bearings, South Dakota, was never finalized, or because he's still seeing Miss J.M., even after having sworn to you that it's finally, definitely over?

Your husband is accommodating his desires just fine, thank you. Obviously, the real issue isn't your fatigue or your lack of sexual appetite (both perfectly normal—and temporary—at this stage of pregnancy). Since no legitimate therapists practice in your area, we suggest that together, you make a toll-free call to a syndicated radio shrink and straighten out this morass of a marriage before bringing a baby into it.

PIT-STOP ANXIETY

It seems like I need to pee every fifteen minutes. It's embarrassing, especially at work or when I'm in mixed company. Why is this, and when will it stop?

Mindee recalls that early in her first pregnancy, she was presenting a paper to the Society of Molecular Physicists, Atomic Engineers, Nuclear Chemists, and Guys That Clean Lab Sludge Wearing Rubber Gloves. Halfway through, she had to pee so badly, she couldn't go on. Clever Mindee spontaneously made as if she needed a glass of water to demonstrate a point about hydrogenated oxygen. She made a beeline to the bathroom, quickly relieved herself, and brought back her "prop." No one was the wiser. So in tricky public situations such as this, you must rely on your wit. And at work, see if you can swap desks with whoever is closest to the facilities.

Just why this problem exists in early pregnancy, is, um, something to do with fluids and liquids and some spigot near your kidneys. You might get a brief reprieve from "pit-stop anxiety" in your second trimester, until such time as the fetus's growing skull begins to exert unbelievable pressure on your bladder.

CAN I FACE LIFE WITH STRETCH MARKS AND SPIDER VEINS?

I've worked hard to maintain a toned body and I enjoy showing it off in scant swimwear when my husband and I travel to Cozumel and Antigua, or when I visit my lover, Eduardo, in Baja California. I expect to get right back into shape after I give birth, and okay, it sounds shallow, but is there any way to prevent stretch marks and spider veins?

Many pregnancy guides will tell you to think of these pregnancy scars as badges of courage or medallions of motherhood. Blah! If you have the means, consult your cosmetic surgeon—you have our blessing. And Bonnie wants to know if by some chance, your lover Eduardo's last name is Rodriguez-Hernandez-Smith. If so, please pass along her regards and tell him that her heart still beats faster every time she recalls those torrid, moonlit nights in Baja.

• •

THE NESTING SYNDROME:
Exactly what will it cost you?

The hormonal upheaval of pregnancy triggers a little-used portion of the female brain that has survived the millions of years since the evolution of our species from pterodactyls. These dinosaurlike birds were the first creatures to act upon the urge to "nest"; in other words, to prepare a proper home in which to hatch their giant eggs. Though we've evolved, pregnancy still sets off that urge to "feather our nest" in anticipation of a new family member. The nesting syndrome brings out our instinct to:

❑ …scrub the house spotless from top to bottom.

❑ …turn the spare room into an adorably wallpapered nursery.

❑ …redecorate the entire home, from frilly attic-window valances to a quilted furnace cozy.

❑ …have all necessary infant items ready, so that the baby can feel secure when it is brought into a well-equipped home.

The prehistoric pterodactyl, the earth's first "mama bird"

Unfortunately, what was once as simple as preparing a basic layette of cotton clothing, diapers, and a few wooden toys has turned into a consumer's worst nightmare. A baby born today will go through more clothing, equipment, supplies, and toys in its first two years than it will for the rest of its life, even if it lives to be 100.

We hoped to help you weed through the incredible number of baby products out there. But sadly, we couldn't find anything to leave out. Your only hope is if you've been salting away lots of cold, hard cash for this baby-having venture. It costs more to raise a baby for six months than it does to open a bookstore-café or start a telecommunications empire!

We must now switch to a much smaller type size for our list of basics, so it doesn't go on forever—we have lots more valuable advice to fit into the paltry few pages our publisher allotted us for this book.

Baby comb and brush	Changing table	Lullaby tapes
Baby cosmetics	Crib	Medicine spoon and dropper
Lotion, powder, oil,	Crib bedding, 3 sets	Mobile, black-and-white
shampoo	Crib bumpers, 2	Mobile, colorful, musical
Baby toys, basic: activity center,	Crib mattress	Nasal aspirator
rattles, plastic keys, etc.	Curtains, nursery	Night light
Bassinet	Diaper pail	Outfits, various sizes,
Bath towels hooded, 4	Diaper bag	2 to 3 dozen
Bathtub, infant	Diaper wipes	Outerwear (jackets, coats)
Bears, teddy, 4 or 5	Diaper covers, 8	Pacifiers, 3
Blankets:	(if using cloth)	Play-mat, travel
Receiving, 3	Diapers, initial supply	Quilt, decorative, for
Fleece, 1 or 2	Dresser	wall above changing table
Crib quilt, 1 or 2	High chair	Rocking chair
Booties, 3 or 4 pairs	Humidifier	Stretchies, a dozen or so in
Bouncer seat	Infant car seat	various sizes
Bottles, 6 to 8	Infant front-pack carrier	Tape recorder, child's
Bottle warmer, travel	Infant nail clippers and scissors	Teething rings
Bottle nipples, 8	Infant seat	Thermometer, digital
Breast pump	Infant swing	Toy chest, decorative
Bunting	Lamp, cute, for nursery	Undershirts, two dozen
Carriage-stroller	Light switch, decorative	Wallpaper, nursery

This list contains only what you will need for the first six months. It does not begin to touch on baby's later needs, including a playpen and walker, scads of six-months-and-up toys, and shoes that are outgrown in one month but which cost double what yours do; after all, we don't want to panic you unnecessarily.

So, what's the bottom line? Assuming you get about half of these items as gifts (see "Making Sure Your Baby Shower Is Memorable and Profitable," page 87); you will need about $9,657.75 for the first six months' needs. See? It's not so bad. But if you feel faint, sit down and put your head between your knees. Then take a few deep breaths and consider these two additional clever strategies:

❑ Get chummy with a mother of young children who doesn't plan to have any more. Women who've been through it all are generous about handing down clothes and equipment to friends who need them.

❑ Start compiling your birth announcement mailing list. Did you know that "birth announcement" is a secret code word for "gift solicitation"? Everyone's a sucker for them, and a good-sized mailing of about 1,000 names will net you at least $3,000 worth of gifts, even with a minimum 25 percent return rate. Increase the announcement's effectiveness further by including a reproduction of the baby's precious footprint!

Part Four

4

THE SECOND TRIMESTER

THE OBSESSED: ME, MYSELF, AND I

EXPECT THE UNEXPECTED AT YOUR SECOND TRIMESTER PRENATAL CHECKUPS

The second trimester is typically devoted to an intense interest in yourself—your physical and emotional feelings, your burgeoning figure, and the acceptance that there's something growing inside of you, and it ain't a turnip.

Let your second trimester exams reflect this self-obsession. The prodding and testing of the first trimester visits is over, and the intense anticipation of birth is yet to come. There's not much to do during this trimester's visits aside from the obligatory urine tests to check for too much starch (or is that sugar?). As a result, most of your time can be spent bombarding your practitioner with oodles of questions—"What's this blotch on my leg?" "Why am I still nauseous?" "What year was the Treaty of Guadalupe Hidalgo signed, ending the United States' war with Mexico?" "Can't I have just *half* a cigarette?" Don't be embarrassed—no question is too preposterous, and there's nothing your practitioner hasn't seen or heard before. Not even:

"Is it my imagination, or is there something going on between us?" At this stage, many women grow attached to their male practitioners, and a small minority even fall in love. If this is the case for you, be smart and keep it to yourself. You look foolish enough as it is in those disposable paper gowns without making an even bigger idiot of yourself.

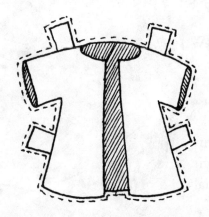

Disposable paper gowns have been named "most humiliating female garment" by Women's Wear Daily *every year since 1945, except in 1972, when paisley tube tops won this dubious award.*

What You Might Look Like This Trimester

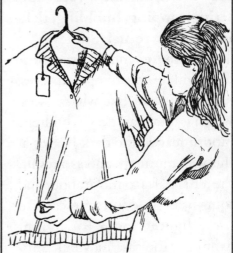

Hungry you! Your appetite is bottomless. You even hate to go to sleep at night, because that means eight hours without food!

You'll soon be making the transition from "fat clothes" into maternity wear.

$ $

IRWIN GLICK'S TAX TIPS FOR THE SECOND TRIMESTER

❑ Milk, milk, milk! Aren't you sick of drinking so much milk? But you do it because you know it's good for your body. Likewise, charitable contributions are good for your soul—and the bottom line of your taxes. What? You say you can't afford to make them? How about buying a couple less designer outfits, or forgoing a month or two of facials and manicures?

❑ Leg cramps and fetal activity keeping you up nights? Don't waste time tossing and turning. Use the time to catch up on your reading. I recommend *P. K. Messer's Guide to Your Retirement in the 21st Century and Beyond.* It will provide you with hours of useful entertainment.

SECOND TRIMESTER MILESTONES

Hey mom, it's me—your fluttering, tapping, bubbling, tickling little fetus! Somewhere around the twentieth week, the fetus will be able to open its eyes. And it will not like what it sees, which is total darkness. Children's inborn fear of the dark begins at this very moment, and as a result, the fetus starts to move about and squirm, in an effort to escape to some lighter room (or lighter womb, as the case may be). Supposedly reputable pregnancy manuals call these first movements by their true scientific name of "quickening," from the Latin *quikus inim*, meaning "Who turned out the lights?"

How do you distinguish these thrilling fetal movements from what was once charmingly called "stomach dyspepsia"? First fetal movements are commonly described as one of the following sensations:

Rapping or tapping, as if the fetus is trying to knock on a door

A burst of bubbles

Fluttering, like a butterfly

A feather, as if the fetus is tickling you internally

Did I hear a WOOSH-slosh?
The excitement of hearing your baby's heart beat for the very first time ranks second only to bungee-jumping into the Grand Canyon. You'll be treated to this wonderful sound with the aid of a Doppler device. This is a sort of hand-held megaphone that, in conjunction with a clear, cold jelly, conducts sound waves out of your abdomen. Hey, don't ask for any more details, we didn't invent this gizmo.

Expect the unexpected! Your baby's heartbeat will not sound like an adult's heartbeat in miniature (ba-**BOOM**, ba-**BOOM**, ba-**BOOM**); rather it sounds like someone running rapidly through slush in galoshes: **WOOSH**-slosh, **WOOSH**-slosh, **WOOSH**-slosh.

Help! The reality is sinking in!
The only down side resulting from the thrill of actually feeling and hearing your baby is **SHEER AND ABSOLUTE UNBRIDLED PANIC!** Here's a small sampling of reactions that some women have after the initial high of these experiences:

❑ "My God! There's a tiny person trapped inside me!"

❑ "Help! I'm going to turn into my mother!"

❑ "Oh, I wish I had gone to Nepal and Tibet when I had the chance!"

❑ "How am I going to take care of a baby? I barely remember to water my plants!"

❑ **"EEEEEEEEEEEEEK!"**

Don't worry. These feelings are normal (slightly neurotic, yes, but still within the normal range), but greatly exaggerated, as emotions tend to be during pregnancy. If you experience this type of panic, just make yourself two or three nice, big, nutritious sandwiches, pour yourself a quart of milk, and plop in front of "Oprah" for a while. We guarantee you'll feel much better once you distract your body with a protein-digesting stupor.

This is so important to know that you should read it and commit it to memory at once!

YOUR FIRST FASHION CRISES

● ●

THE RAPIDLY VANISHING WAISTLINE

Somewhere between the third and fourth month, your figure will go from looking like an hourglass to looking like a drinking glass. Then, that fateful morning will come when your favorite jeans just won't zip up. This is the time to make the transition to "fat clothes," which include elasticized pants and skirts, oversized tops, and the father-to-be's nicest sweatshirts.

MAKING THE TRANSITION FROM "FAT CLOTHES" TO MATERNITY WEAR

Right around the fifth month, you'll begin straining the elastic of those "fat clothes." And you'll feel obligated to explain to everyone, even people who don't know you, that you really *are* pregnant, not just fat. The problem is, you're not quite big enough to fill out maternity clothes. They make you look like a three-year-old in a sailor dress.

If you're self-employed or unemployed, you can hide at home wearing your "fat clothes" during this brief transitional period. But if you need to look decent for work, you can use one of those "pregnancy poufs" for a month or so (you know, those foam things that models strap on to look pregnant); these will make your dress-for-success maternity outfits look more proportional.

Don't worry—before you know it, you'll be filling out maternity clothes with the best of them.

THE UNDERPANTS DILEMMA

If more women could foresee "the underpants dilemma," perhaps there would be fewer pregnancies in this world. You see, your regular bikinis or high-cut hipsters just don't work with a ballooning belly. So you'll have to decide: Are you going to take the "under-the-belly" approach, and buy those string bikinis worn by women with names like "Blaze," or are you going to take the "over-the-belly" approach and buy great big underpants like the ones Grandma Gilda Glick wears?

OKAY, LET'S GET IT OVER WITH—A CHECKLIST OF TODAY'S MOST POPULAR PREGNANCY COMPLAINTS

Some women will have just a couple of them, others will experience the whole gamut, and most will fall somewhere in-between. But everyone loves to complain about them. What are we talking about? Symptoms, of course—physical and emotional. But wouldn't it make them more bearable if you knew that each one of these nuisances actually contributes to the beauty, well-being, or character of your baby? Really! It's true!*

YOUR SYMPTOM	HOW IT MIGHT BENEFIT YOUR BABY
Fatigue	Baby will be the "spirited" sort who will initially wear you out, but will ultimately become a successful go-getter
Constipation	Baby will master toilet-training at an early age
Dull headaches	Baby will have useful right-brain skills like the ability to watercolor, speak French, and make a perfect omelet
Absent-mindedness	Baby will grow up with left-brain dominance useful for math, astronomy, and chess

*Of course, this is a crock of nonsense. However, we thought if you could be convinced that your discomforts have value to the baby, they might be more endurable.

Mood swings	Baby will possess a rich, unrepressed emotional range
Clumsiness	Baby will be fearless, never afraid of adventure and risk
Palms and bottom of feet are red	Baby will have healthy, ruddy coloring
Heartburn	Baby will be blessed with a charitable spirit and strength of character
Indigestion	Baby will be a good eater, and may even be open to eating vegetables
Swelling of ankles, feet, and fingers	Baby will have a round, ticklish belly
Varicose veins	Baby will grow up to be athletic, with a chance for a combined athletic/academic scholarship to a private college
Nocturnal leg cramps	Baby will be a graceful dancer

THE MYSTERY OF WEIGHT GAIN

In *Seven Swelling Wives for Seven Swell Brothers,** Ma Jessup says that most women gain between twenty-five and thirty pounds during pregnancy. We beg to differ. Our informal survey of several dozen pregnant women puts this figure at a solid thirty-five to forty-five pounds.

We *do* agree with Ma Jessup that the average baby weighs seven and a half pounds at birth. But how is the remaining weight gain accounted for? Using our thinking caps, we came up with a precise breakdown of a forty-four-pound weight gain, much like Mindee's during her last pregnancy:

Baby:	7.5 pounds
Placenta:	1.5 pounds
Bavarian creme donuts:	8 pounds
Cheese and/or cheese-flavored snacks:	10 pounds
Miscellaneous afterbirth substances:	2 pounds
Chocolate foods (M & M's, truffles, milkshakes, etc.):	9.5 pounds
Water accumulation in puffy feet, ankles, and fingers:	4.5 pounds
Total:	**44 pounds**

* An old western novel Mindee bought at a yard sale for our research—the original 1949 edition by Wiley "Howdy" Taylor—what a find!

WHAT YOU MAY BE FRETTING ABOUT

• •

OLD WIVES TALES

My Slavic grandmother says that if I wear a bag of garlic around my ankle during pregnancy, it will protect my baby from "the evil eye." Is this true?

In these high-tech times, it's easy to dismiss old wives tales as twaddle. But if there's nothing to them, why have they persisted for centuries? Take "the evil eye"— every culture on the face of the earth fears it, though no one has ever really seen it, let alone knows what it is. Somehow, it quietly persists in letting us know that it may be in our neighborhood.

We're talking about protecting a baby here, so why take chances? Be a good girl and listen to your grandmother. Wear a bag of garlic around *both* ankles. You can always hide them with an attractive pair of boots.

Fifty years from now, CD-ROMs, electronic bulletin boards, voice mail, and all that kind of stuff will probably be obsolete, but the same "old wives tales" will still be around. We be-lieve that hidden wisdom lurks in all 13,300 of the known superstitions relating to pregnancy and birth. Here are just a few of our favorites:

❑ If you carry high and pointy, it will be a boy. If you carry low and wide, it will be a girl.
—*Lithuania*

❑ If you carry low and wide, it will be a boy. If you carry high and pointy, it will be a girl.
—*Bulgaria*

❑ If a rooster crows at the moment of conception, your baby will grow up to be an attorney.
—*U.S. (Nebraska)*

❑ Don't kick or curse at a pig while pregnant, or your baby will be born with a foul temperament.
—*Isle of Wight*

❑ If you dream of an Elvis impersonator while pregnant, your water will break a week before your due date.
—*U.S. (Tennessee)*

HOW YOU MIGHT BE "CARRYING," SIXTH MONTH

Women "carry" their pregnancies in many different ways, all of which invite an unbelievable amount of unsolicited commentary from friends, family, and strangers. Prepare to be annoyed by comments like, "You're carrying so big / so small / so high / so low / so pointy / so flat!"

Carrying big

Carrying small

Carrying pointy

Carrying flat

SAMPLE SNAPPY COMEBACKS FOR COMMENTS ON HOW YOU'RE CARRYING

Carrying high

Coming from left field as they do, these comments can leave you stammering for a smart answer, which you will think of three hours later, when the offender has moved on, often to another state. Look at the pictures here and decide how *you* are carrying. Then, prepare a snappy comeback that will leave the insensitive commentator, not you, with a gaping jaw. Here are a couple of ideas to get you started:

Insensitive person: You must be due any second—you're carrying so low!

You: Actually, I'm not due for another two months. But my husband and I conceived on his workshop table in our basement, and ever since, "junior" just seems comfortable being as close to the ground as possible.

Insensitive person: Gulp.

Or another:

Insensitive person: So, when are you due?

Carrying low

You: Next month.

Insensitive person: That soon? You're carrying so small to be due next month!

You: Well, I had a fling with a pygmy chieftain when National Geographic sent me to the Belgian Congo for a photo shoot.

And you must remember from your Social Studies classes that pygmies are among the lightest and most compact of the Peoples of the World.

Insensitive person (turning deep red): Oh, I uh, mumble, mumble…

SONOGRAMS AS PREDICTORS OF YOUR CHILD'S FUTURE TEMPERAMENT

Sonograms are not only a neat-o way to peep in on what the fetus is up to, they are also a way to peer directly into your future child's *soul.* Observing the fetus's behavior in utero can give you a valuable preview of the personality that will someday emerge.

The Devil with a Baby-Doll Face: *This imp is already in training for "the terrible twos." You might want to start moving breakables to the top shelf at once!*

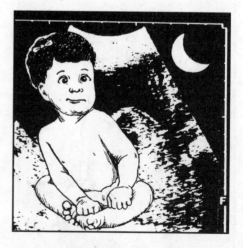

The Night-Owl: *Uh-oh. This fetus is quiet by day, and just starts hitting its stride at nightfall. Expect to spend the next couple of years on the night shift!*

Little Red Running Shoes: *This fetus is in perpetual motion, kicking, squirming, never resting for a moment. You're going to need a good pair of running shoes yourself to keep up with an inevitably active baby and child.*

The Womb-Potato: *Languid and lazy, this fetus gently moves about and stretches now and then. You can expect one of those rare, easygoing children who loves to sleep and amazes fellow travelers with his or her good behavior on transatlantic flights.*

Nervous Nell (or Nervous Neil): *Every little noise makes this fetus jump. Rather than kick and stretch, it twitches and jerks. This is an omen of a high-strung, nervous personality.*

Class Clown: *This baby-to-be is already smiling, and occasionally chuckling, as if enjoying a private joke. This one's first words could well be "knock, knock."*

QUIZ: SHOULD YOU GIVE BIRTH AT HOME, LIKE OLIVIA DE HAVILAND IN *GONE WITH THE WIND,* OR AT THE HOSPITAL, LIKE BARBRA STREISAND IN *THE WAY WE WERE?*

You are not merely a Pregnant Person, you are a Childbirth Consumer! You have choices! This quiz, though comprised of gross stereotypes and fraught with tired clichés, will nonetheless help you determine the most suitable place for you to give birth.

You are a good candidate for home birth if you...

❑ ...live in rural Idaho or Montana, or any other place that's more than 150 miles from the nearest hospital.

❑ ...dread being seen in public in those ridiculous hospital gowns, and disdain the thought of having to eat highly processed, nutrient-free hospital food.

❑ ...enjoy growing bean sprouts in jars, tending your compost heap, and making your own dulcimers.

You should think about using a birth center if you are...

❑ ...a slightly new age-y, quasispiritual person who uses botanical cosmetics and drives a rugged, all-terrain vehicle.

❑ ...a person who believes that a woman's natural ability to give birth is enhanced by a homey setting, so long as it's not *your* home that will get drenched with birth glop.

❑ ...convinced that you need only relaxation techniques, breathing, massage, scented pillowcases, and a mantra to get you through birth.

You should definitely give birth in a hospital if you are...

❑ ...a Jell-O freak.

❑ ...a technology buff.

❑ ...a person who knows yourself well enough to admit that you couldn't possibly get through childbirth without major drugs, and the closest you'll ever get to natural childbirth is doing it without makeup.

• •

OTHER CHOICE LOCATIONS IN WHICH
TO GIVE BIRTH

LOCATION	PROS	CONS
In the car on the way to the hospital	At least you get it over with quickly	There goes the upholstery
In an airplane	Flight attendants always act as if they know exactly what to do	Other passengers annoyed by screaming infants
On public transportation	Your baby's birth gets lots of local media coverage; cops who help get to be heroes	Complete lack of privacy
In the wilderness	As close as you'll ever get to truly natural birth	Shrubs and grasses can be prickly; difficult to clean up afterwards

This is so important to know that you should read it and commit it to memory at once!

HORMONAL THUNDERSTORMS

• •

This scenario will be familiar to anyone who has been pregnant: One minute you're sitting there calmly, minding your own business, when suddenly, some minor incident transforms you into an irrational, raving maniac. These emotional explosions, blamed on an obscure hormone called L-Triptogen, are so intense that they can turn even veterans of military combat in the Third World into cowering, sniveling wimps.

| *Not even this…* | *could ever prepare you for this.* |

Our comments will now be directed to the fathers-to-be. Listen, guys, we're not looking to cast blame here, but it's been proven that 92 percent of all hormonal thunderstorms are caused by unintentionally thoughtless fathers-to-be. Okay, so you may be genetically predisposed to certain careless acts, but be aware that in conjunction with a Pregnant Person, this behavior can have devastating results. Some examples:

❑   Scheduling prolonged visits from children of your previous marriage(s) on weekends when you have to work.

❑   Not lying convincingly enough when your wife asks whether you think she looks fat and gross.

❑   Transferring half of your savings into risky biotechnology stocks or soybean futures.

❑   Rearranging the furniture as a "surprise" for her. Pregnant women do not take well to having their "nest" disturbed.

Remember to wear your "consideration caps" at all times, fellas. And take some comfort in knowing that not all of her hormonal thunderstorms are your fault. The remaining 8 percent are caused by:

❑   The evening news—all that violence and tragedy makes her wonder about the kind of world she is bringing a child into. But even a crummy weather report can send her into a hormonal tailspin.

❑   Sad country music, tragic operas, and right-wing radio talk-show hosts.

❑   Documentaries of live birth—they either make her highly emotional or scare her senseless.

MORE FRETTING

• •

I'M AFRAID I'LL CHOKE ON MY PRENATAL "HORSE PILLS!"

My prenatal vitamins are the size of large water beetles. Each day, I live in fear of taking them. What good is it going to do me to be pregnant if I'm just going to choke to death on these "horse pills"?

As far as we know, there have been no recorded deaths as a result of choking on prenatal vitamins. Don't be tempted to crush them into small pieces; they splinter into razor-sharp shards that are extremely painful to swallow, as Bonnie once found out the hard way. Mindee was lucky enough to have access to a molecular compressor at her lab, which shrank her vitamins to a comfortable size, but this is not the kind of equipment the average person has around the home.

All we can say is, be brave and take your "horse pills." Yes, they are cumbersome, but you need the vitamins and iron for your growing baby, not to mention some of the other important min-

erals such as uranium, plutonium, cobalt, bauxite, and charcoal.

THE MANY FACES OF PREGNANCY

I admit it—I feel like heck. I've got every symptom under the sun, and my husband says that all I do is complain. But my friend Debbie feels fabulous, and in her sixth month, still manages to turn heads when she walks down the street (though to me, she looks like a furnace in drag). Why are our pregnancies so different?

The way your pregnancy shapes up is a result of your basic personality plus hereditary factors, divided by the frequency of your mother's phone calls and your mother-in-law's insidious comments. Everyone is a certain "type" during pregnancy. You sound like a classic "Kvetch," and your friend Debbie fits the profile of the "Earth Mother." But don't worry, dear. Our own Bonnie was "Kvetch from Hell," and now she is a fairly passable mother. Here are the most common pregnancy types:

The Kvetch: She's a walking smorgasbord of symptoms: lower back pain, tender gums, heartburn, constipation, hemorrhoids, swollen feet, stretch marks, varicose veins, skin blotches, and leg cramps—you name it, the Kvetch has it. Even the "uneasy queasies" are with her to the very end. After her family and friends tune out her constant kvetching, she starts complaining to anyone who can be a captive audience, like twenty-four-hour catalog phone-order operators, people behind her on supermarket lines, and hard-of-hearing neighbors.

The Earth Mother: She's one of those infuriating gals who never feels as vibrant, as healthy, and as sexy as when she is pregnant. She wears form-fitting bathing suits proudly over her enormous belly and never consumes empty calories or refined sugar. If she has any minor aches, she doesn't complain, because for her, pregnancy is the world's most empowering experience. She radiates such well-being that the Kvetch and the Worry-Wart would love to slap her senseless. Only her sensitive partner as labor coach and sparkling water—no narcotics!—will sustain her during a totally natural childbirth.

Who Me? Pregnant? Too busy for symptoms, this efficient, energetic mother-to-be conceals her condition until her eighth month by wearing loose, but well-tailored suits. Her pregnancy comes as a complete shock to her co-workers (or as is usually the case, her subordinates, since she either owns the company, or is at least the boss). "Who Me? Pregnant?" will give birth on a Thursday, right after work. This gives her three full days to recover and break in the nanny before returning to work on Monday.

The Totally, Helplessly Obsessed: True, very few expectant mothers (apart from Who Me? Pregnant?), aren't obsessed with their pregnancies, but the Totally, Helplessly Obsessed takes the cake. She can't stop talking about herself and is constantly rubbing her belly, as if she's polishing a bowling ball. At the drop of a hat, she'll whip out her collection of sonogram pictures and point out the baby's toes.

Evenings will find her poring over her vast trove of pregnancy literature, occasionally regaling her mate with minutia like: "Oh! Our baby is 6.7 centimeters long today!" or "Oh! Our baby got its fingernails in today!" or "Oh! Our baby learned how to count to five in Spanish today!"

The Totally, Helplessly Obsessed can't understand why everyone else isn't as fascinated with her condition as she is—she has convinced herself that she is the world's first pregnant woman, breeding the world's first, ultimately perfect infant.

Part Five

5

THE THIRD TRIMESTER

NATIONAL

WILDLIFE

TUSKED ELEPHANT

STRIPED BEHEMOTH

AFRICAN HIPPO

MOBY-DICK

WARTHOG

Enormous Mammals Issue

LIVIN' LARGE

EXPECT THE UNEXPECTED AT YOUR THIRD TRIMESTER PRENATAL CHECKUPS

Zzzzzzzzzzzzzzz, snore. Zzzzzzzzzzzzzz, fidget, grumble. Oh, sorry! We dozed off while figuring out what to say about third trimester prenatal exams. You see, just thinking about them is a real yawner. What was a novelty at the beginning of your pregnancy is now becoming a chore, now that your visits are increasing from once a month to twice a month, then weekly. And if they are such a bore for you, the pregnant person, think of how deadening it must be for us to write about them.

Expect to become irritated with your practitioner's office decor, and to have memorized the contents of the magazines in the waiting room. Bring your own reading material.

Expect raised eyebrows and muffled snickers from the nurses when you're being weighed. This won't happen in reality, of course, but in your current state, you are highly prone to hallucination.

Expect a lot of internal and external manipulation. You'll be told if the baby is right-side up, upside-down, sideways, or backwards. You'll be given guesstimates of how much it weighs, how big its head is, what gender it is, and whether it is sucking its thumb. Why bother to give birth? Some practitioners give away all the surprises before you even go into labor.

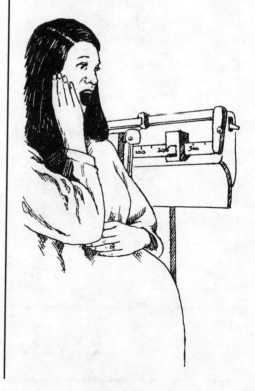

What You Might Look Like This Trimester

OH, HONEY!
COULD YOU HELP
ME OUT OF
THE TUB?

Your girth complicates everyday activities that you've always taken for granted, like getting out of the bathtub.

You begin to obsess over the impending birth. Sometimes, you are so spaced out that it's impossible to get your attention.

$ $

IRWIN GLICK'S TAX TIPS FOR THE THIRD TRIMESTER

❏ Just because you lose a little urine each time you sneeze, you don't have to lose control over everything in your life. For instance, why have a baby in January, and lose the benefit of having a brand-new dependent for the year you spent being pregnant? A little planning goes a long way: Conceive no later than March 15 so you can deliver the baby in the same tax year.

❏ Being pregnant makes you feel immortal, as you nurture the new tax dependent within. But someday, you will kick the bucket, just like everyone else. Don't leave your precious heirs out in the cold—call your Tax Professional at once to update your will.

WHAT YOU MAY BE FRETTING ABOUT

• •

THE EMPATHY FACTOR

I want to kill my husband when he tells people that "we're" pregnant. I know he does it because he's bursting with pride, but he's not the one who had to put up with three months of nausea, whose body is rapidly being taken over by another being, and who will soon endure childbirth. How can I make him stop without hurting his feelings?

We agree that, while extremely annoying, there's no malice intended here. Men say things like this simply because they are dear, simple-minded lugs, and because most of them don't know their elbow from an atom ionizer (Mindee contributed that clever analogy).

So rather than trying to explain to him with short words that he is *not* pregnant by any stretch of the imagination, it is better to show him, using the following "empathy techniques."

❏   Have him strap something around his waist that weighs about twenty pounds (such as a large watermelon, an antique typewriter, or a humidifier) and wear it to work.

❏   Make him a hero sandwich piled with sauerkraut, jalapeño peppers, and an assortment of salty, highly processed lunch meats. Serve with pork rinds and cheap domestic beer. This will produce the worst case of heartburn he's ever had.

❏   Attach lead weights to his ankles and have him put on shoes that are two sizes too small. This simulates your swollen feet and ankles. Then, send him for a brisk, five-mile walk.

❏   To simulate the constant pressure on your bladder, have him drink several gallons of juice or water daily, so that he will have to take a leak at least every twenty minutes.

❏   Get him to go through his daily routine without once bending at the waist.

❏ For forty-eight hours, have him refrain from cigarettes, alcohol, junk food, coffee—in fact, anything that gives him bodily pleasure. We don't include sex here, because you've probably already trained him to go without it for far more than forty-eight hours.

Put a stop to this "we're" pregnant business now or, when the time comes, your mate might stride into the hospital and announce to the medical staff that "we" will definitely not need any painkillers!

If the father-to-be agrees to do any three of these five empathy exercises, we guarantee that he will not only stop saying "We're pregnant," but he will begin to give you sad, kindly looks, and even take up a few of the household chores that men don't normally think to do. However, don't expect this practice to continue much beyond the baby's delivery.

HEY YOU! GET OFF OF MY BLADDER!

The baby's head is now in the downward position, and its precious little skull is exerting constant pressure on my bladder. Is there any relief in sight?

Well, of course—giving birth solves this problem at once. Not only will the baby's head be separated from your bladder, and, indeed, sometimes be in a different room than your bladder, but you will forget all about this crushing discomfort once your body replaces it with the aches and pains of postpartum.

In the meantime, try the following: Prepare a strong broth

made of onions, garlic, and dried Italian mushrooms. Taste it; you probably won't like it. Discard into sink. Then, put on a tape of the Righteous Brothers' greatest hits and dance, as best as you can force yourself, with gyrating motions. When you need to rest, look at a coffee table book about traveling in Franz Josefland, and read some passages loud enough for the fetus to hear. Finally, drive to the nearest betting parlor and place a trifecta bet.

This series of random activities may cause the baby to lift its head in confusion long enough to give your bladder a brief reprieve.

COME ON NOW, ARE MEN *REALLY* TURNED ON BY PREGNANT WOMEN?

I've heard tell that men find the pregnant body sexy, sensuous, and a real aphrodisiac. I find this hard to swallow. I feel about as sexy as the Hindenberg. What's the truth?

The notion that men are turned on by pregnant women is merely a rumor that got blown way out of proportion. Partners of women in their childbearing years are, by and large, in their twenties and thirties. Guys in this age group go mad with testosterone poisoning if forced to go more than three days without sex. And somewhere along the line this blind lust was misinterpreted as a genuine desire for the pregnant body. No one has dared to deny this rumor until now, since no one likes to upset hypersensitive pregnant gals and perhaps even trigger a hormonal thunderstorm (see page 60).

Now here's some advice from your friends Mindee and Bonnie (Eunice wouldn't touch this one—she strongly disapproves of sex during the third trimester): the power of aphrodisia rests in the mind, so if you can make yourself believe that you really *are* sexy and sensuous, inflated though you may be, perhaps your partner will believe it too.

Try this approach, then write to us and let us know how it turns out. And give lots of glorious details—our readers would like to hear more about this burning issue than our own scant experience can provide. Right, Mom?

1,001 WAYS (WELL, JUST SIX) TO AVOID HAVING SEX IN LATE PREGNANCY

The hows (and whys) of having sex become an intense obsession in late pregnancy. "Brand X" pregnancy manuals, which devote many pages to the subject, all say that couples should go for quality (rather than quantity) sex at this stage. Bonnie and Mindee seem to understand this, but I, Eunice, don't get it. How can you have "quality" sex when almost every position is at best, awkward, and at worst, incredibly goofy?

You preggies love statistics, so here goes: The odds that you will have quality sex in your third trimester are .0067 per thousand, and your chances for having quantity sex are 75 percent less than that. In other words, quality, shmality, quantity, shmantity. Your chances of having hot, steamy sex with Bob Seger music blaring in the background are now close to nil.

Mindee and Bonnie wanted to come up with suggestions on improving late-pregnancy sex, but I put my foot down and said "no!" The girls whined and said, "But, why?" and I answered calmly, "Because I'm still your mother, and I said so." After all, you have the rest of your life to have sex, and you can resume a perfectly wonderful love life once your youngest child is sleeping through the night, at age seven or so.

I was left on my own to recommend ways to avoid sex, because my spoiled, selfish daughters wouldn't help. I would expect it of Bonnie, but Mindee's behavior was totally out of character. And I apologize, since I could only think of six strategies, but if you put your mind to it, you can probably think of some others yourself.

1. Say that you *must* see whether Sam and Diane are going to tie the knot on "Cheers," even though this is the umpteenth time you've seen this episode in syndication.

2. Tell him that you're still angry that he didn't stand up for you when his mother said something to the effect that you're hardly fit to walk in his dust, much less care for his progeny.

3. Spend your nights burning midnight oil to finish the novel that's been stuffed in the bottom drawer of your desk since you were in college.

And for him:

4. Channel your testosterone bursts into other macho pursuits. If your wife sends you signals that she's in the mood, pretend that you are very busy polishing your rifles or oiling your socket wrench set.

5. Sublimate your sexual desire into creative pursuits. Try needlepoint, crewel, embroidery, or painting on velvet. While doing these kinds of things, your wife will never think of you in a sexual way.

6. Use the classic male excuses: that you're afraid you'll "hurt the baby" with your fearsome manhood, or that you have this odd feeling that someone, i.e., The Baby, is "watching."

How the heck are you supposed to have sex when even a simple kiss is so much trouble?

BUT IF YOU REALLY, *REALLY* MUST...

I, Eunice, could talk myself blue in the face, but I have enough sense to know that most of you can't be talked out of your hedonistic urges. So, if you and the daddy-to-be really, *really* must satisfy them at this late stage, I approve only of sex that involves no physical contact, such as that time-honored classic, phone sex.

You can take this concept further and have fax sex, fax/modem sex, voice-mail sex, answering-machine sex, and e-mail sex. Try some of these contact-free positions—they may actually expand your erotic horizons in ways you never dreamed possible. If you're not completely satisfied, write to me and I will send you my Aunt Malka's famous rum babka cake as a consolation.

And now, this section on sex will be concluded (thank goodness) with a somewhat off-color cautionary tale, which is unfortunately true—honest to gosh!

A friend of Mindee's was a week past her due date, when someone informed her husband that having sex could help induce labor. Since his wife hadn't been keen on making love at all for some weeks, the dimwit naturally assumed that this meant having sex with someone else. So, on his way home from work that day, he stopped off to have sex with an old girlfriend. Then he went home and told his wife about it, hoping that it would help bring on labor.

Well, it worked. The shock made her water break with the force of Niagara Falls, and she had their baby five hours later. After she was back on her feet, she served her husband with divorce papers.

Mindee's friend went on to win the Pulitzer Prize in literature, became a wealthy novelist, and married a sensitive, equally wealthy import/export magnate. They had three more children, all geniuses. The ex-husband's old girlfriend, on the other hand, turned out to have many screws loose, and he went bankrupt paying for her regression therapy and psychoneuro-immunology treatments.

An extreme case, perhaps, but if this helps keep partners of the very pregnant on the straight and narrow, then it's well worth the paper it's printed on, don't you think?

**This is so important to know that you should
read it and commit it to memory at once!**

FROM EXTRA-LARGE TO TITANIC:
Solving the Fashion Crises of Late Pregnancy

• •

Ah, vanity. Even the very, very pregnant woman wants to look her best. But it's a monumental challenge to dress a body that has ripened from womanly fruit into the mutant produce of those awful 1950s horror movies. Here are the most common fashion dilemmas you will face, and simple ways to deal with them.

The protruding belly button crisis: *If your third trimester falls in the warmer months, sheer or thin fabrics, bathing suits, and light colors call attention to this protrusion. Nothing seems to disguise it, and small children are always trying to "beep" your belly.*

Solution: *Adopt a sporty look by wearing binoculars (a camera will work, too) around your neck. Your belly button will be well disguised, and you will create an air of mystery as those around you wonder what you're searching for.*

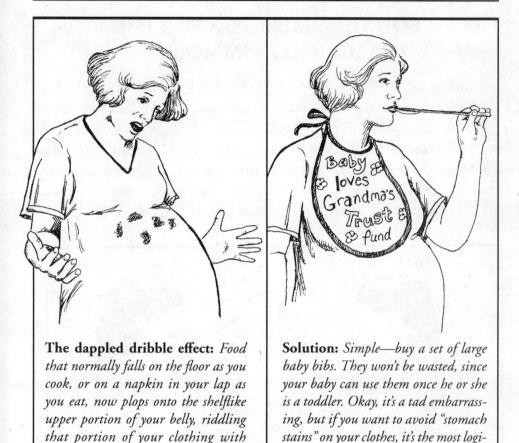

The dappled dribble effect: *Food that normally falls on the floor as you cook, or on a napkin in your lap as you eat, now plops onto the shelflike upper portion of your belly, riddling that portion of your clothing with stains.*

Solution: *Simple—buy a set of large baby bibs. They won't be wasted, since your baby can use them once he or she is a toddler. Okay, it's a tad embarrassing, but if you want to avoid "stomach stains" on your clothes, it's the most logical thing to do.*

The outgrown maternity clothes dilemma: You're in the stretch—in more ways than one: You've got four, maybe six weeks to go, and your maternity clothes no longer fit. Everything is bursting at the seams, but you really don't want to invest in any more huge maternity outfits this late in your pregnancy. What can you do?

Solution: Slipcovers solve most any decorating crisis, and since they have little adjustable strings here and there, they're just the thing for this fashion crisis, too. And—you can always buy a coordinating window swag to use as a scarf or a wrap. After you deliver, you can use the slipcovers to protect your furniture from spit-up stains.

BONNIE'S EXERCISES FOR THE PRACTICALLY IMMOBILE

When Bonnie was in the eighth month of her first pregnancy, her doctor took her to task for gaining too much weight. And all that excess poundage caused her to stagnate: Once it took her an hour and a half just to get up off the sofa. After weeping for a week, Bonnie resolved to scale back on the Ding Dongs and Slim Jims and to embark on a program of gentle movement so she wouldn't become completely immobile. If Bonnie could do these exercises, anyone can. Go to it!

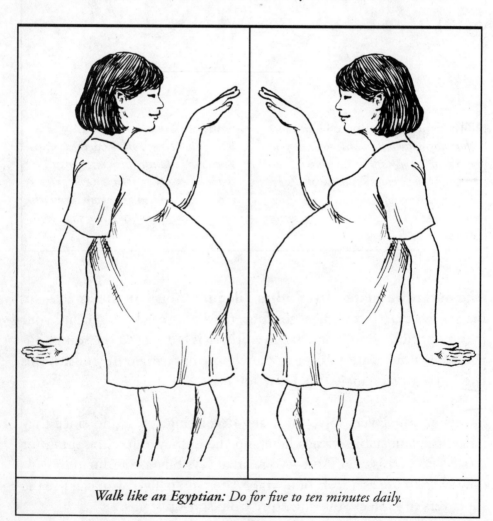

Walk like an Egyptian: Do for five to ten minutes daily.

Waddle like a duck: *Do for three to four minutes, three times daily.*

Stand like a colonial home: *Stand this way for five minutes, once in the morning and once in the evening.*

Lightweight lift: *Lying on your left side, lift this book high in the air thirty times. Have someone help you turn to your other side, and repeat with another thirty lifts. If you can, do this exercise in the display window of your local bookstore—we'd really appreciate it!*

THE BELLY PAGES:
When Your Belly Becomes Your Universe

• •

> ### Belly—as obstacle

Check the boxes as the following "no-can-do's" happen to you:

❑ Can't sleep on belly anymore

❑ Can't fit behind the steering wheel

❑ Can't remember how your toes look, let alone clip your toenails

❑ Can't tie shoes without great effort or help

❑ Same goes for putting on socks or pantyhose

❑ Can't turn over in bed; if you want to roll from one side to another, you actually have to sit up and heave yourself over

❑ Can't get up from a sofa or easy chair without help

> ### Belly—as public property (see also Unwanted Advice, page 86)

Why would a total stranger come up to you and rub your belly? Tradition has it that this brings good luck to the person doing the rubbing. The same type of person often throws in a piece of totally unsolicited advice for good measure, leaving you good and aggravated. We think you are perfectly within your legal limits to practice any of the Oriental martial arts on belly-rubbing strangers.

Belly button, protruding

See Fashion Crises of Late Pregnancy (page 76).

Body parts, baby's: Identifying through belly

This is one of the most fun (or bizarre) aspects of late pregnancy. Turn off the TV. Sit on the sofa next to your mate. Now look at your belly and try to guess what body part is kicking or bumping out from your belly. The challenge is to learn to distinguish a hand from a foot, an elbow from a knee, or—a real toughie—the head from the tushy.

Contractions—Hackensack-Bricktown—in belly

Imagine that there's an invisible string tied around your protruding belly button. Now imagine that someone pulls gently and firmly on that string until all the muscles in your belly are tightly bunched up. That's what Hackensack-Bricktown contractions feel like. The purpose of this strange, yet painless phenomenon is to prepare your body for the Real Thing.

Hiccups in belly

What are those funny spasms you're feeling? Could it be? Yes, Baby has a case of hiccups, and is letting you know! Drinking a glass of water won't help these hiccups, but drink the water anyway; you need the fluid.

CHOOSING THE LEAST WIMPY AND CLICHÉD NAME FOR YOUR BABY

The third trimester finds parents-to-be preoccupied with the business of finding just the right name for Baby. Saddling your child with your gene pool is something over which you have no control, but condemning him or her to live with an unsuitable moniker is a different matter—what could the parents of Ima Hogg have been thinking about?

Numerous fascinating yet highly unscientific studies have shown that names affect how people feel about themselves, how others perceive them, how much money they will make, and even what kind of car they will drive. Who do you think is more likely to drive a Jaguar, a Camilla or a Prunella?

Here are some common approaches for naming babies. If most of our opinions are directed toward boys' names, it isn't because we favor the Stupider Sex, it's only because boys' names are more problematic.

The traditional (or cliché) approach: By far the most popular method for naming babies, this involves selecting a name that has been run into the ground through centuries of use. Take Michael, for instance. One would think that more than enough Michaels have passed through our planet, yet this continues to be the number one name for boys.

If you are really intent on taking this approach, why not at least consider an alternate spelling? This has already been done with wildly successful results with girls' names—plebeian Karen becomes Caryn, plain Alison becomes Allyson, and simple Amy becomes romantic Aimee. The same tactic can be used to make traditional boys' names more distinctive. Try turning Michael into Mykelle, John into Jonne, or David into Dayvidh.

The wimpy approach: It's amazing that so many baby-name books warn parents-to-be against naming their boys "Percy" lest the child be beaten up by classmates. While we basically agree, we also feel that the name "Percy" has

Often a child's personality grows to "fit" their name. Look at these two boys. It should be easy to tell which is Derek and which is Peabody.

been unfairly singled out for wimpiness. There are many other, even wimpier boys' names that should be avoided:

Peabody	Smedley
Bartholomew	Aloysius
Egbert	Poindexter
Ebeneezer	Mortimer

The heritage approach: The age-old tradition of naming the child, usually a boy, after his father, who was named after his father, and

so on. This approach works best if you are from old money and the baby's name turns out to be Philip Charles Livingston III, or the like. But if the father's name is something like Billy Ray Butkus, the Heritage Approach is not for you.

The surname approach: If you've exhausted all the possibilities in the baby name books, choosing a name that's more commonly a last name is a unique approach. This can be used for both boys and girls, and the baby will grow up with a name that has a certain clout.

Many famous people have surnames as first names, like Jackson Browne and Mackenzie Phillips. Sometimes reversing first and last-type names works splendidly, too, as it does for Morgan Brittany and Elton John. Use common sense with this method, though. Don't name your baby "Smith" if your last name is "Jones." And avoid giving a daughter *too* masculine a name. Lincoln, for instance, is a great surname-as-first-name for a boy, but not for a girl.

Finally, the majority of surnames just don't work as first names. So please, no matter how much you love this book, don't name your baby "Glick."

The rock star approach: This is one to avoid—it involves giving your baby the most outlandish name you can come up with. Only people with colossal egos and/or major substance abuse problems would inflict names like "Moon Unit," "Dweezil," or "Zowie" on their children.

The riffle-through-the-name-book-in-the-hospital approach: A surprising number of parents-to-be can't agree on a name even after the baby is born. It's not unusual to hear of cases where hospitals refuse to release the baby until it is named, since some name must go on the birth certificate. So, the dog-eared baby name book is pulled out once again, and thus, a lot of babies named Adam, Andrew, Abigail, and Andrea are born.

SOME TIPS ON NAMING GIRLS

Finding interesting names for girls is generally easier than it is for boys, but beware of these pitfalls:

❏ Old-fashioned names like Mildred, Clarabelle, and Bertha are fine for great-aunts, but can you imagine them for a two-year-old? "Mildred! I said do *not* paint the kitty!"

❏ On the flip side, some names are fine for two-year-olds, like Trina, Tammi, and Tabitha. But can girls with such precious names aspire to upper management in major corporations?

❑ We recommend strong, exotic names like Natasha, Savannah, and Ebony. But be careful not to give girls the wrong kind of exotic names, such as Scarlett, Fawn, or Chérie, which might cause them to become strippers when they grow up.

❑ Don't name your daughter after a virtue, like Patience, Hope, or Chastity. Women have enough trouble growing up in this day and age without that kind of pressure.

HOW A CHOICE OF NAME MIGHT AFFECT YOUR DAUGHTER'S LIFE

Mildred

Tammi

Chérie

Patience

MORE FRETTING

• •

HOW TO AVOID AGGRAVATING THE VERY, VERY PREGNANT

Now that I'm so obviously pregnant, it seems like everyone in the world has advice, nervy comments, and birth stories for me. I wish they'd all mind their own business and leave me alone. Am I being too sensitive?

You poor dear. Women in the late stages of pregnancy are tired, impatient, and uncomfortable. They need a lot of TLC, and the last thing they need is to have the following Four Cardinal Sins of Very, Very Late Pregnancy perpetrated on them:

Unwanted advice: Whether you are a friend, foe, relative, or stranger, don't give the Very, Very Pregnant advice unless she asks for it. A huge belly is not the equivalent of a sign that says, **"I NEED SOME CHEAP ADVICE AND I NEED IT RIGHT NOW!"** Nothing could be further from the truth.

Comments on their girth: Our cousin Brenda, who carried big and recently had a strapping, healthy boy, reports that shortly before she was due, a man approached her and said, "Wow! I guess when you get to be as wide as you are tall, you can pop any time!" And this was certainly not an isolated incident. Exactly what was it this man's business how big Brenda was? Don't make comments like this to the Very, Very Pregnant. We have spies everywhere; we will find out and we will make you sorry you opened your big mouth.

Horror stories: Some experienced moms have an uncontrollable urge to share their labor and delivery "war stories" with their pregnant friends. Don't you think this is a tad cruel, especially directed at a first-time mother-to-be? If you were going to have brain surgery, would you want to hear about that isolated case when the doctor accidentally lobotomized the patient? Think before you blab.

Remarks on passing their due date: Nothing irritates the Very Very Pregnant like constant calls to find out whether she's given birth. Remarks like **"WHAT? YOU'RE STILL HERE?"** when she's seen at work or out and about, with belly still in tow, are equally unwelcome. Believe us, no one is more anxious than the Very, Very Pregnant Past Her Due Date. She doesn't need you to further fuel her impatience, and yes, she *will* let you know the minute she's given birth. Or so she says, as a handy way to get rid of you.

MAKING SURE YOUR BABY SHOWER IS MEMORABLE AND PROFITABLE

This might sound cold and calculating (and it is), but is there any baby-shower equivalent to a "bridal registry"? Just as with my wedding gifts, I want to make sure my friends get quality gifts for my baby, and not just some cheap, tacky stuff that I could probably afford myself.

Sorry, but baby-shower registries are extremely rare. Still, you can ensure a profitable baby shower by telling your friends that you have your heart set on a "theme party." Be direct and ask for the classic "bigger-than-a-bread-box" theme, to which everyone has to bring a gift that is, you guessed it, bigger than a bread box.

Since no one would knowingly deprive a pregnant woman of her heart's desire, this method is a sure-fire way to get the big-ticket items on your wish list (see The Nesting Syndrome: Exactly what will it cost you? on page 38): bigger-than-a-bread-box items like infant carriers, car seats, strollers, playpens, swings, and the like.

And make sure to "ooh" and "ahh" appreciatively over all your splendid and expensive baby gifts.

I DREAM OF BABY

Vivid dreams are a hallmark of pregnancy. Some are peaceful and pleasant, and some are strange, as dreams often are, reflecting the uncertain feelings of the mother-to-be prior to giving birth.

❑ A dream about multiple birth either means that you feel overwhelmed—or is an omen that you will have twins!

❑ Many women dream of having kittens or puppies instead of a baby. This symbolizes confusion about your identity as a mother. Or, it is simply a weird dream.

❑ Dreaming that the baby's father is a man of great genius, like Pablo Picasso, indicates a great desire for your child to be a super-achiever. Mindee had one such dream about her idol, Albert Einstein. Bill Gates and Wolfgang A. Mozart are other favorites in this type of dream.

MAJOR SCHOOLS OF THOUGHT ON MANAGING LABOR PAIN

Here's some information to take with a pound of salt—these methods of easing labor pain were all invented by men! What do you know about that! Is it any wonder, then, that in all of their literature, pain is referred to as "discomfort"? If men were the ones giving birth, they'd spend a lot more time inventing safe, pain-numbing drugs than coming up with stylized breathing techniques. Here's a rundown of the top four techniques and their philosophies:

Headly-Dick Mountbatten British school of Edwardian psychogenesis	Concentrates on relaxation techniques, discourages medication
The Amazing Bradlee American school of "White Magic"	Concentrates on relaxation techniques, discourages medication
La Bouyant water method French school of aquatics	Concentrates on relaxation techniques, discourages medication
La Marz rhythmic breathing method of "painless childbirth" Austrian school of deep breathing	Concentrates on relaxation techniques, discourages medication

PROFILE: GUSTAVE LA MARZ, INVENTOR OF "LA MARZ BREATHING":

Savior of Laboring Women or Deranged, Cigar-Chomping Lunatic?

Gustave La Marz was the eldest son of an itinerant Austrian couple. His father, a gambler with a wandering eye, and his mother, a gypsy with a wandering soul, schlepped their eight children from village to village, performing in their family yodeling show.

Gustave, an intellectual, bespectacled boy, was humiliated by being part of this travesty. He retreated into books that he begged, borrowed, or stole whenever he could.

Gustave La Marz

One evening, as the teenaged Gustave was reading a book about Pavlov (the scientist who conditioned dogs to salivate at the sound of a bell) a windstorm howled outside the family's tent: Shh, Shh, SHOOOOSH; Shh, Shh, SHOOOOSH. Gustave's mother, in labor with her ninth child, called to him, "Gustave! Come help!" as his father was, as usual, out gambling and womanizing. The boy resented being snatched from his reading, but he helped his mother deliver the baby, as he had done many times before.

Years later, La Marz broke away from his family and was adopted by a prosperous couple. He became a respected obstetrician, but never quite recovered from his unstable childhood. Always haunting him was the confused memory of that night his mother gave birth, the book about Pavlov, and the wind—Shh, Shh, SHOOOOSH.

One day, while treating a particularly nervous patient and chomping on a cigar (La Marz was a cigar addict and was rarely seen without one) he had a major "AH-HAH!" If labor-phobic women could be conditioned to breathe in a funny way, like, Shh, Shh, SHOOOOSH, they would be diverted from screaming. Then, La Marz reasoned, he could convince the world that he had invented "painless" childbirth. How brilliant! He would become famous and rich, rich, rich!

And so began a massive and brilliant PR campaign for the "La Marz Breathing Method for Painless Childbirth," resulting in the greatest hoax ever perpetrated on womankind. Every night for the rest of his life, La Marz chomped on his cigar and cackled with maniacal laughter as he thought of millions of Pavlovian women, Shh, Shh, SHOOOOSH-ing in response to labor pain. Only he, and legions of laboring women knew the truth about this alleged "painless childbirth," but no one has dared admit to it, even to this day.

• •

WHAT TO EXPECT FROM YOUR "CHILDBIRTH PREPARATION" CLASSES

Right about the time when your belly causes a total eclipse of your view of your large toes, your practitioner will urge you to take a series of childbirth preparation classes. The purpose of these classes is to obliterate any remaining shred of humility or modesty you may still be hanging onto, which may inhibit a successful childbirth.

In these classes, you will engage in such activities as passing around plastic wombs and rubber babies while nodding and smiling; lying on the floor in a bovinesque position, pretending to hyperventilate; and having other couples stare at you and your partner, trying to imagine what you might look like when you have sex.

In short, these classes will prepare you for birth about as effectively as juggling lessons would prepare you for an earthquake.

This is so important to know that you should read it and commit it to memory at once!

TRAINING YOUR "LABOR COACH," A CUSHY, OVERRATED JOB IF EVER THERE WAS ONE

• •

The labor coach is supposed to assist you through the labor and delivery process, but more often than not, becomes a big pain in the neck. This exalted job is usually given to the father-to-be, primarily to bolster his ego and give him something to do during labor and delivery aside from behaving like a maniac. The duties of a labor coach should be limited to:

❑ Helping time the contractions

❑ Driving the woman to the hospital or birth center

❑ Filling out forms upon arrival

❑ Holding the woman's hand or head during contractions, breathing with her, and saying, "You're doing great, honey!"

Most labor coaches shouldn't attempt anything more than this, or they will cause mass confusion. One well-meaning father-to-be, a therapist, mistook his wife's pain for hostility and began analyzing her. Needless to say, this didn't sit well with her, and she slapped him and told him to just shut up and breathe.

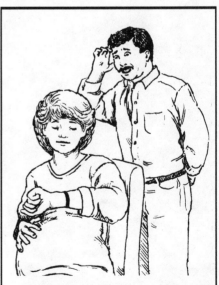

Labor coaches can be helpful in timing contractions if they are not too nervous or upset and want their mommies.

Try not to be too annoyed by his endless mantra of "You're doing great, honey!" It's the only thing he can think of saying.

The best thing to do with a labor coach is to get him back to his usual routine as quickly as possible.

Part Six

6

LABOR AND DELIVERY

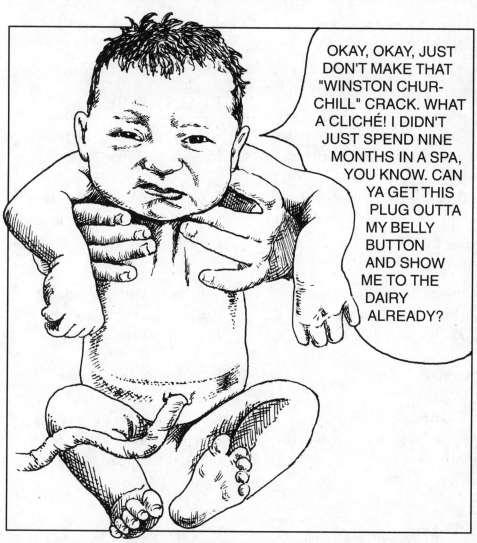

WHY IT'S CALLED "LABOR" AND NOT "PARTY TIME"

You're almost at the finish line, you fertile filly! Racing to the end, you are now in the throes of anticipation of labor. There is a rather fine line between labor and prelabor that first-timers have trouble distinguishing. How can you tell the difference, and thus avoid the crushing disappointment of being told that you are experiencing "false labor" and sent home from the hospital?

IT'S THE REAL THING: HOW TO TELL FALSE LABOR FROM REAL LABOR

FALSE LABOR	REAL LABOR
You can fuss over your hair and makeup between contractions	You no longer care what the hell you look like
You call your best friend and tell her you think you're going into labor	You can't remember your best friend's name, let alone her phone number
You're having abdominal discomfort because you had shish-kebab for dinner	You couldn't eat a bite for dinner, so this can't be an ordinary tummy-ache
Your dog sleeps	Your dog howls
Contractions feel as if you've been hit with a tractor-trailer	Contractions feel as if you've been hit with a tractor-trailer full of the Sunday *New York Times*
It's 2:00 P.M. and you can still wait to call your practitioner	It's 2:00 A.M. and you can't delay calling your practitioner a moment longer

IMPORTANT TERMS YOU'LL NEED TO KNOW WHEN YOU GO INTO LABOR

Back labor: We prefer to refrain from making remarks about a topic that distresses so many women.

Breech delivery: We're not qualified to comment on topsy-turvy births.

Ceasarean Section, or C-Section: We refuse to be drawn into making snide, satirical remarks about C-Sections. That would be tasteless—this is major abdominal surgery! We prefer to limit our snide, satirical remarks to vaginal birth only.

Contractions: You'll know when you're having them; you don't need us to paint pictures for you.

Demerol: No comment.

Dilation: Never mind.

Enema: Don't ask.

Epidural: This one we'll talk about. The number-one most beloved labor drug today, the word epidural comes from the Greco-Roman *epi* ("makes labor") *dural* ("endurable"). In just a few minutes, you can go from riding waves of merciless contractions to refreshing your lipstick and reading magazines. But whether to use it is a very personal matter, and we refuse to advise you about it one way or another.

Episiotomy: Another topic that would be tasteless to discuss. We abstain from commenting on a procedure that is universally disliked by women.

Forceps: You couldn't pay us to give you our opinion on this one.

Pitocin: We can tell you that pitocin is a drug used to induce or rev up labor, but we won't tell you what we think of it. We *will* tell you what our cousin Rhonda said, which was "NO!!! Don't turn up that dial!"

VBAC (Vaginal Birth After Cesarean): Too controversial—we wouldn't touch this topic with a ten-foot pole.

WHAT YOU MAY BE FRETTING ABOUT

STILL SQUEAMISH ABOUT LABOR

The big day is almost upon me. Even after taking good care of myself, all the childbirth preparation classes, and a positive attitude, I'm still nervous as all get out. Tell me the truth—is labor really as awful as it's cracked up to be?

If we said "Oh, yes, it's every bit as hideous as you've heard, and then some," would you turn back the hands of time, knowing you've come so far? We won't lie and say that labor will be one of the high points of your life, but how awful can it be, if almost every woman is willing to go through it again, and sometimes repeatedly, often even *intentionally?*

Some say a sort of "birth amnesia" makes women forget labor pain once they bond with their sweet babies. Nonsense! No one forgets a single second of their entire birth experience; and not one of the 6,987 women interviewed for this book said they would decide against having a second child just because labor isn't as much fun as an Eric Clapton concert. Even Bonnie, the world's prize weenie, was ready to get pregnant again a year after her first baby was born, even though we warned her not to have any more children with Mr. Wanderlust.

WHEN YOUR WATER BREAKS IN PUBLIC

I live in fear of my water breaking in public. Any tips?

Why should you be ashamed of a little amniotic fluid? Okay, so sometimes it seems like gallons and gallons of fluid, but that's only an illusion. This is just another sexist injustice—men are allowed to spit on every curb, but pregnant women are made to feel embarrassed about their sacred water bag.

However, if the thought of public gushing makes you uncomfortable, here are some effective "camouflage" techniques to use if your water breaks...

...at the supermarket: Get a gallon of apple juice and smash it on the floor over the same spot where your water broke. Then get the manager and apologize profusely for making a mess of the apple juice.

...at work: Similar technique, only use the water cooler. If anyone asks you why you were trying to carry the water cooler to your office, just say that women on the verge of giving birth need lots of fluids.

...at a formal social occasion: Wear a floor-length gown with a full skirt wide enough to hide the fluid on the floor beneath you. Stand in the same spot until everyone else goes home.

...at an awards ceremony: If, for instance, you're accepting the Nobel Prize in physics (as Mindee hopes to do shortly) or the Academy Award for Best Screenplay, just admit what has happened—you couldn't pay for such great publicity! You could say that you are so honored and excited to get the award that your womanly riverbanks have overflowed. The media will have a field day!

I'D LIKE TO THANK THE MEMBERS OF THE ACADEMY, AND...OMIGOD!!!

WHAT'S ALL THIS FUSS ABOUT THE PLACENTA?

From time to time during my pregnancy I've heard talk about the placenta. Delivering the placenta, burying the placenta, and whatnot. I'm about to have a home birth. Is there something I should know?

There *is* an awful lot of emphasis on "delivering the placenta," as if it's an instant sibling for the newborn. The placenta's exalted status is due to the fact that it helps nourish the fetus. Among many traditional societies, the placenta is buried after childbirth in the belief that it will fertilize the soil. Actually, the newborn infant has sapped the placenta of any value it once had.

Somehow, this ritual has been adopted by certain crunchy granola-headed people in our own society. You know, the kind that drive ancient VW vans and listen to the original soundtrack of the Woodstock concert on *turntables,* for heaven's sake! If this sounds like you, have a nice ceremony if you must; bury your placenta while reciting poems about the Mother Goddess. But please, don't give your placenta a name, and don't plant mums over the spot in which it is buried—they won't survive. Plant rhododendrons instead.

WHAT TO TAKE TO THE HOSPITAL

● ●

❑   A couple dozen copies of this book, to be passed out to other laboring moms-to-be in need of diversion.

❑   A picture of an adorable niece, nephew, or puppy, or a really cute mandala, to use as your "focal point" when you need intense concentration.

❑   A portable tape player with earphones and a selection of great, rhythmic music to labor to. Mindee highly recommends Peter Gabriel's *SO* album, which has not only a driving beat, but also songs appropriate to the occasion, like "Sledgehammer," and "Don't Give Up."

❑   "Brand X" pregnancy manuals always suggest bringing a tennis ball to use for back massage, but we think a soccer ball is far more effective.

❑   Makeup, lotions, powders, shampoo, conditioner, mousse, toothpaste, dental floss, and other cosmetics. You'll never actually use them in the hospital, but packing them will give you something to do in the early stages of labor.

❑   Lots of literary novels and political magazines like *New Republic*. You won't have the patience to read anything, but if you arrange this literature casually on your night table, the hospital staff might take you for someone with brains, and not treat you as condescendingly as they do other patients.

❑   Don't forget an outfit for yourself to wear home; one of your earlier "fat outfits" with elastic still intact will fit you best after giving birth. Bonnie's sister-in-law forgot to bring an outfit to wear home, and she had to leave the hospital wearing a caftan the size of Cleveland.

**This is so important to know that you must read it
and commit it to memory at once!**

WHY THE HUSBAND IN ALL THOSE OLD MOVIES WAS ALWAYS SENT OFF TO BOIL WATER, AND OTHER GREAT MOMENTS IN CELLULOID BABY-HAVING

• •

Did you ever wonder why, after the kindly old doctor arrived on horseback in old movies, the hysterical husband was always instructed to go and boil up a great big pot of water? The answer is simple—back in the old days, husbands weren't needed to drive the woman to the hospital, since most women gave birth at home. Neither were they used as "labor coaches." In fact, everyone preferred to keep the husband as far away from the birth scene for as long as possible. And boiling a huge pot of water was a great way to keep them busy. Lighting a primitive stove or building a fire took time, too, ensuring that the husband was out of the picture for several hours.

It's hard to believe, but cinematic birth is even more ridiculous than it is in real life. Here's a random sampling:

The Postman Always Knocks Up Twice: This is where that cliché about the baby being "the postman's" originated (or is it "the milkman's"? Oh, well...). A steamy thriller about an amorous mailman who impregnates two women on his route and then is murdered. Which of the two jealous husbands killed him?

THE POSTMAN ALWAYS KNOCKS UP TWICE

The Way We Weren't: Opposites attract as passionate, Jewish Katy and cool, WASPish Hubbell fall headlong in love, as proven by the obligatory canoeing-in-the-park scene. Unfortunately, by the time they realize that they're fatally mismatched, Katy is about to give birth. When Hubbell comes to bid Katy farewell at the hospital, all he can say about his new daughter is, "She's so...little." Then he leaves her to raise the child alone while he takes up with a model. Somehow this is depicted as being all right, if only a tad sentimental.

Gone for Good With the Wind: At the end of this four-hour Civil War saga, Rhett and Scarlett finally part ways after she nixes the possibility of any more pregnancies. After all, her waist has already expanded to twenty-one inches from its original nineteen when the story began. This spells doom for the couple, for whom sex was the only bond, much as it is for Bonnie and her husband (who possesses Rhett's snakelike qualities, minus the charm and looks). Most memorable line: "But, Miz Scarlett, I don't know nuthin' about birthin' babies!"

• •

THE STAGES OF LABOR: OHHHHHH, UGHHHHHH, AND ARGHHHHHH!

Early labor, or OHHHHHH, is characterized by:

❏　Contractions five to twenty minutes apart that feel like mild to moderate smacks by a waffle iron.

❏　A husband who hides his terror by fiddling with a Swiss stopwatch.

❏　The need to put the finishing touches on your "nesting syndrome," with activities like hanging up the baby's developmentally correct black-and-white mobile or installing a nice set of vertical blinds.

❏　The desire to walk for fifteen miles or take a four-hour bath.

During active labor, or UGHHHHHHH, you can expect:

❑ Contractions that measure 8.2 on the Richter scale.

❑ A husband who busies himself by helping you breathe between trips to shove your hospital things into the trunk of your car or a cab.

❑ To be admitted into the hospital or birth center, if that's where you're going; or if you're giving birth at home, having the midwife arrive and install dropcloths all over your house.

❑ To feel like laughing when seeing your husband in surgical scrubs that make him look like an actual doctor, especially if he was once rejected by every medical school to which he applied.

❑ To be angry at nurses who keep telling you to lie down, even though this is the world's most uncomfortable and ineffective labor position.

During pushing and delivery, or ARGHHHHHH! you can expect:

❑ Contractions that feel as if your feet are firmly planted on either side of the San Andreas fault, when it suddenly splits and forms a twenty-foot-wide chasm.

❑ In some cases, to say unthinkable things to your husband, either because you've had it with his saying, "You're doing great!" for thirty-six hours, or because you blame him for the state you are in. Warn your husband in advance to disregard whatever you say during "transition" —particularly if you make him promise to marry your newly divorced best friend if you don't survive childbirth.

❑ To be told to resist the urge to push by panting like a dog for a few minutes, so that the hospital's birth attendants can go to a quick meeting.

❏ To be told, finally, to push. Women have one of three reactions to this command: 1) Most will try to push. 2) Some will refuse. In this case, husbands will have to resort to bribery and promise expensive gifts, such as jewelry, to inspire their wives to push the baby out. 3) The third reaction, more common than you'd think, is to scream for a C-section. Come on, ladies! Would you also scream for open-heart surgery during a routine physical? Be a big girl and push that baby out already!

AUTO PILOT: A FEW TIPS ON MAKING IT TO THE HOSPITAL IN ONE PIECE

Don't even think about making the trip in a fifteen-year-old vehicle with a leaky transmission.

A motorcycle is perfect if you need to maneuver to the hospital during rush hour in Los Angeles.

SHH, SHH SHOOOOOOSH, SHH, SHH SHOOOOOSH

A race car is a very sensible choice of transportation, though not very roomy if you need to give birth en route.

Finally, if you must take a cab, use a medallion vehicle and not a "gypsy cab," and make sure before getting in that the driver knows sufficient English to understand the difference between *Mount Sinai* Hospital and *Montsini* Pizzeria.

MORE FRETTING

● ●

CROWDS IN THE DELIVERY ROOM

There seems to be a trend for women to have their mother, some friends, their plumber, and various childbirth instructors present when giving birth, especially in birth centers. I'm not sure I want a lot of people to watch me, but I also hate to miss out on current fads—I even bought a few pairs of bell-bottoms recently when it looked like they were making a comeback.

Just thirty years ago, not even the father-to-be was allowed to watch his wife give birth, but nowadays, the entire neighborhood wants to come and gawk.

Childbearing as a spectator sport began in eighteenth-century France when scalpers sold tickets to the public to view the birth of Marie Antoinette's son, the future king. After falling out of favor for two centuries, this practice was revived by childbirth instructors who can only be described as "birth groupies." Even after having had six babies themselves,

they just can't seem to get enough of the birth experience, and so, invite themselves to the births of their "instructees." Once the families and friends of laboring women get wind that some no-account childbirth instructor is going to be there, they insist on coming, too.

Hey, it's your birth. Who you invite or don't invite is entirely up to you, and you shouldn't feel pressured by fads and trends. And that goes double for those bell-bottoms.

IS IT REALLY SUCH A GOOD IDEA TO HAVE YOUR BIRTH VIDEOTAPED?

A friend of mine wants to attend my birth and videotape it. Isn't that cool? Are there any tips or rules of etiquette I should convey to her?

Bonnie thinks that videotaping births is a swift idea (this opinion comes from the same exalted mind that thinks lip-piercing is a wonderful trend, too), but I (Eunice) and Mindee are a bit more squeamish on the subject. If you were having root canal, would you want that to be videotaped, also? All right, so root canal can in no way compare to the miracle of childbirth, but neither is it nearly as messy.

If you feel compelled to have your birth videotaped, at least give your cameraperson the following guidelines. These tips apply to taking photos with a still camera as well.

❑   Don't allow strobes or other high-intensity photo lights. Laboring women themselves throw off so much heat, that this additional wattage could cause the cameraperson and other spectators to combust.

❑   In unmedicated births, don't allow any footage to be taken of you during "transition."

❑   Tell your cameraperson to watch where they aim. Bonnie's friend Paula had a video person who kept zooming in on her private parts at odd moments, unknown to her. Weeks later, when they showed their birth video to her husband's skiing buddies (with popcorn and all!), these shots caused Paula extreme mortification.

Watch where you aim, cameraperson!

A CHILD IS BORN

● ●

1. Baby feels the rumblings of the first contractions; wakes up cranky and hungry, as infants usually do.

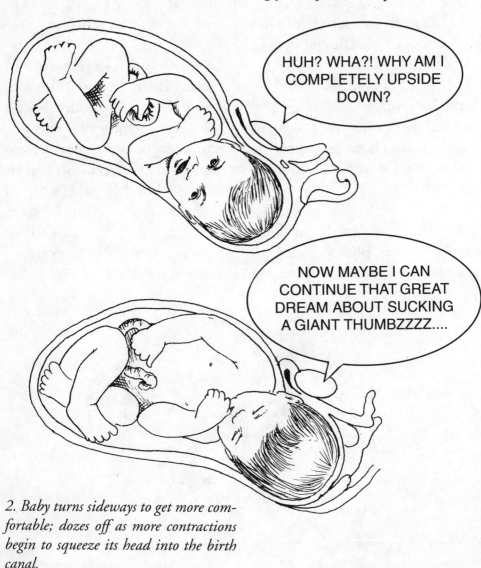

2. Baby turns sideways to get more comfortable; dozes off as more contractions begin to squeeze its head into the birth canal.

3. Baby is woken up by a massive contraction and head begins to "crown."

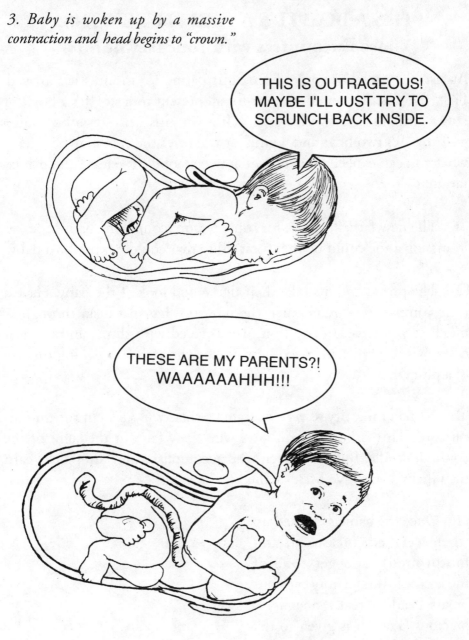

4. Baby's head and shoulders emerge; the rest of the body squeezes out like toothpaste from a tube.

IT'S A BOY! IT'S A GIRL! IT'S TWINS!
Close Encounters with Your Newborn(s)

At last, the moment you've been anticipating for months has arrived. First, the practitioner announces for all present to hear, "It's a boy!" or "It's a girl!" or "It's two boys!" or "It's two girls!" or "It's a boy and a girl!" or "It's two boys and a girl!" or whatever the case may be. Here's what you can expect after the initial two seconds of release and exhilaration:

❑   The new father always, for some reason, counts the baby's toes, as if missing a toe could be the worst thing that could happen to a baby.

❑   The proud parents take their first, good look at the baby. Have a little compassion—remember, the newborn has just been through as much as you have. In addition, it is covered with slime, and in most cases, has its grapefruit-sized head forced through an opening the size of a plum.

❑   A small minority of very liberated fathers will now cut the umbilical cord. This is not for you guys who grew faint at the sight of the epidural needle. But those men who accomplish this daring deed earn the Glicks' "Sensitive Male of the Year" award.

❑   Once the baby is cleaned up (then weighed, measured, and footprinted), and gets one of those cute little stocking caps put on its head, it really does look precious. Then it is given to the mother, and the new parents look at it, blubber incoherently with happiness, and begin "bonding."

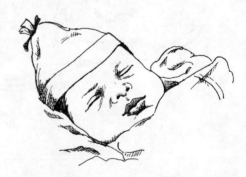

Bonding is thought of as the process by which deep family attachment is formed. However, on a recent archeological expedition to Israel, Mindee unearthed an ancient tablet (archaeology and geology are her hobbies) revealing that "bonding" is a corruption of the word "bondage." We now have proof of what we have known all along—that from the moment of birth and forever after, parents are eternal slaves to their offspring.

• •

BREASTFEEDING BASICS FOR WOMEN WITH ADVANCED DEGREES WHO CAN'T FIGURE OUT HOW TO PERFORM THIS SIMPLE, NATURAL ACT

Picture this scene: a Neanderthal woman is in her cave, caring for her newborn while her mate is out hunting and gathering. Other women in her clan, including her mother, sister, cousins, and the tribe's medicine woman are hovering nearby to care for her and help with the baby. With grunts and gestures, her caretakers ease her into the simple art of nursing her baby.

Today, the scene is radically different. Parents bring their new baby home to relative isolation. Perhaps your mother or mother-in-law will be there, grunting and gesturing, but she will be of little help in the breastfeeding and nurturing departments. In her era, women raised families according to strict societal guidelines, living in boxy houses and wearing shirt-waist dresses. Tragically, millions of years of human instinct were thus totally eradicated.

We are all for breastfeeding—anyone who can should give it a chance. It's healthy for the baby, and great for the mother, who can eat like a Sumo wrestler and still lose weight. Unfortunately, Eunice missed her chance, being of the "June Cleaver" generation. Mindee took her babies to all of her physics conventions and breastfed them until they were ready to nibble on grilled cheese sandwiches. Even Bonnie, who needed a map to figure it all out, finally got the hang of it.

But sometimes, for various reasons, breastfeeding is just not meant to be, and most formula-fed babies grow up to be healthy, normal human beings, contrary to "La Milky Way League" propaganda. New mothers don't need additional guilt to deal with, so all you breastfeeding zealots who nurse your children until they are five, back off!

If you're not yet up to lifting six-hundred-page tomes on breastfeeding (unbelievable though it may seem, women have breastfed their young for millions of years without consulting a single book on the subject!), here are the basic steps:

1. When the baby cries, put your nipple in its mouth and let it suckle for ten minutes, or until the breast is less full and the baby is less hungry.

2. Repeat on the other breast.

3. Burp the baby, then put it, sleepy and content, back into its bassinet.

AND THAT REBECCA THINKS SHE'S SO SMART, AND YAKKETA, YAKKETA, YAK...

This is what you should expect to happen once you get home: While trying to breastfeed your infant, you will need to know when to switch it to the other breast. You flip frantically through the index of your favorite breastfeeding manual, but can't figure out what the subject heading might be. Meanwhile, your mother-in-law, oblivious to your crisis, will blather on about some obnoxious cousin.

YOU'RE NOW THE PROUD PARENTS OF AN ACTUAL BABY THAT YOU'RE GOING TO HAVE TO TAKE HOME EVENTUALLY!

Now what are you going to do?

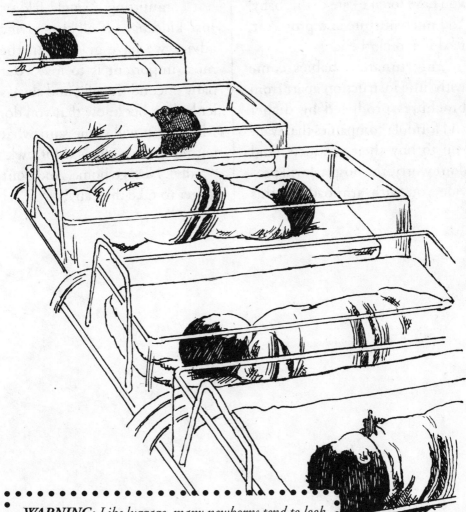

WARNING: *Like luggage, many newborns tend to look alike. Just as you would match your luggage stubs at the airport, make sure your baby's ID bracelet jibes with yours. Otherwise, your family's life will end up being the plot of a made-for-TV movie.*

Congratulations—you did it! You have produced a real, bona fide infant. After the initial "high" of reveling in the wonder of your precious newborn, reality bites—you have to take care of this baby! You must nurture and protect it, feed it and clothe it.

Unfortunately, babies come with little instruction apart from brochures produced by diaper and formula companies that want you to buy their products (and don't worry, the hospital will provide you with armloads of this scintillating literature).

Relax—people with far less education and common sense than you have raised children that have made it to adulthood without committing a single felony! Just kidding. Of all the terrific advice we have given you, the most important is to love your baby unconditionally, and always let him or her know that you do. All the rest will come somewhat naturally (if perhaps a bit awkwardly). Now go home. And don't forget to take the baby!

Bibliography

When we began researching this book, we planned to use only the most up-to-date, technically precise information available. But our resolve soon crumbled as we realized that the highly credentialed M.D.'s, Ph.D's, MSRP's, and so on who write these supposedly authoritative volumes have never been pregnant themselves, and so, haven't the least idea what they're talking about.

However, books were not totally useless to our research. On the contrary, without the valuable insights gleaned from the following books, this would have been just another one of the dozens of stale, repetitious pregnancy guides turned out year after year by those doggone New York publishers:

Nausea by Jean-Paul Sartre

Heartburn by Nora Ephron

Mr. Spock's Baby and Child Care: Breeding, Cloning, and Mutation on the Planet Vulcan by Mr. Spock

The Encyclopedia of Human Existence *(10 Volumes): Pregnancy and Birth; Infancy, the Drooling Stage, and Toddlerhood; Childhood; Adolescence and Early Adulthood; The Period Preceding Middle Age When People Make Pathetic Efforts to Recapture Lost Youth; Resignation to Middle Age; The Retirement Years; Dotage, Death, and Transmigration of the Soul* by the Editors of Human Existence Press

Embroidery for Embryos: Needlecrafts to Make for the Newborn by Gladys Glick

The 100 Funniest Things Midwives Have Ever Said: Jokes and Quotes for Public Speakers and Toastmasters by Harriet Dinnerstein

- *Home Childbirth Practices in the Thatch-Roofed Cottages of Samoa*
- *Lactation in Industrialized Nations*
- *How to Choose a Cozy Nursing Bra*
U.S. General Services Administration pamphlets, numbers 30,007, 36,016, and 42,117

The Agony and the Ecstasy by Irving Stone

Index

ABOUT THE (REAL) AUTHOR/ILLUSTRATOR

Nava Atlas is obviously no expert on pregnancy, but she is considered an authority in the field of vegetarian cooking. An illustrator and graphic designer as well as a writer, her previous books include *Vegetarian Express, Vegetariana, Vegetarian Celebrations,* and *Soups for All Seasons.* She is the owner of Amberwood Press, a book packaging company and small press.

Ms. Atlas used the real *What to Expect When You're Expecting* (which she greatly admires) as the guide for her own two pregnancies. She lives with her husband and two sons in Connecticut.